YOU ARE GOOD AT THINGS

YOU ARE GOOD AT THINGS

AT THINGS

A Checklist

✓

ANDY SELSBERG

A PERIGEE BOOK

A PERIGEE BOOK
Published by the Penguin Group
Penguin Group (USA) Inc.
375 Hudson Street, New York, New York 10014, USA
Penguin Group (Canada), 90 Eglinton Avenue East, Suite 700, Toronto, Ontario M4P 2Y3,
Canada (a division of Pearson Penguin Canada Inc.) • Penguin Books Ltd., 80 Strand, London WC2R 0RL, England • Penguin Group Ireland, 25 St. Stephen's Green, Dublin 2, Ireland
(a division of Penguin Books Ltd.) • Penguin Group (Australia), 250 Camberwell Road, Camberwell, Victoria 3124, Australia (a division of Pearson Australia Group Pty. Ltd.) • Penguin
Books India Pvt. Ltd., 11 Community Centre, Panchsheel Park, New Delhi—110 017, India • Penguin Group (NZ), 67 Apollo Drive, Rosedale, Auckland 0632, New Zealand (a division of Pearson New Zealand Ltd.) • Penguin Books (South Africa) (Pty.) Ltd., 24 Sturdee
Avenue, Rosebank, Johannesburg 2196, South Africa

Penguin Books Ltd., Registered Offices: 80 Strand, London WC2R 0RL, England

While the author has made every effort to provide accurate telephone numbers and Internet
addresses at the time of publication, neither the publisher nor the author assumes any responsibility for errors or for changes that occur after publication. Further, the publisher does not
have any control over and does not assume any responsibility for author or third-party websites or their content.

YOU ARE GOOD AT THINGS

First edition: April 2012

Perigee trade paperback ISBN: 978-0-399-53735-6

PRINTED IN THE UNITED STATES OF AMERICA

10   9   8   7   6   5   4

Most Perigee books are available at special quantity discounts for bulk purchases for sales
promotions, premiums, fund-raising, or educational use. Special books, or book excerpts, can
also be created to fit specific needs. For details, write: Special Markets, Penguin Group (USA)
Inc., 375 Hudson Street, New York, New York 10014.

INTRODUCTION

Sure, we may have lost the masonry know-how to ever build another Chrysler Building. Doctors might no longer make house calls. We can't fix basic plumbing problems without calling a professional. Yet, I look around, and I see so, so many other things people have mastered. And I think, "WE ARE GOOD AT THINGS!"

People often say the world is getting worse, but I say we're getting better. Or at least staying as good as we've always been, which is pretty dang good. We're training cats to ride robot vacuum cleaners. Thousands of folks have mastered the art of getting people to move over a seat in movie theaters. Shouldn't they get a parade? Or something? Where are the congratulations for giving kids names that will never appear on key chains at gift shops, or the accolades for having artful corn-on-the-cob-eating patterns? People need recognition for their unique styles of greatness. Even if we aren't fixing our own cars, building another Notre Dame cathedral, or dressing up for air travel, our talents shine in a million other brilliant directions.

This book is about the skills that don't pay the bills. Everybody's got something special in their wheelhouse, and *You Are Good at Things* is a pat on the back, a flying high five, a proud pair of finger guns in your direction for the things you do that fly under the radar. Like your way with remembering people's allergies, or your ability to insert swear words into regular words. It's about calling positive attention to that friend or cousin who's amazing at differentiating between twins and convincing otherwise reasonable people to play drinking games. Maybe you're good at knowing exactly which historical figures you'd have dinner with. Your ability to unerringly guess the attendance at sporting events may not make it into your obituary, but it's still a pretty impressive knack.

In these pages you will find talents that you and the people you care about possess—talents that have for too long been taken for granted, like your aptitude for remembering to take the leftovers. Check off the skills you've got. Mark the ones you'd like to acquire. Put minus signs next to stuff you wish you weren't so skilled at, like beating yourself up. Take note of what those close to you have the hang of, and be sure to let them know. We all have someone in our orbit who's great at knowing when to break out the leopard print, or a buddy who's mastered four different musical instruments, none of which you've ever heard of. Let's celebrate and remind ourselves of all that we do so well. The sum of these small virtuosities makes humanity human.

This is a song for us, and all our unsung skills. Because seriously: You are good at things.

YOU ARE GOOD AT THINGS

- ☐ Noticing new haircuts
- ☐ Acting surprised when you know it's coming
- ☐ Getting the bartender's attention
- ☐ Telling professional coaches what to do
- ☐ Knowing all the angles
- ☐ Knowing at least one or two of the angles
- ☐ Breaking your own records
- ☐ Making it to the hotel pool before it closes
- ☐ Telling people when they should've dove for it
- ☐ Sensing how many sheets the stapler can handle
- ☐ Reading skywriting before it fades
- ☐ Strapping outdoorsy goods to the top of your car
- ☐ Knowing when spiked collars are menacing and when they're just fashion
- ☐ Adjusting paper airplanes to improve aerodynamics
- ☐ Keeping book club discussions focused on the book
- ☐ Pretending to go to work every day after you've been fired
- ☐ Getting out of bone marrow donation requests
- ☐ Counting down the days
- ☐ Scoring backstage passes

☐ Knowing just how high you can toss a baby before it gets dangerous

- ☐ Finding bars to do pull-ups on
- ☐ Being an angry loner
- ☐ Getting kids to share their toys
- ☐ Getting adults to share their toys
- ☐ Uncorking wine without mangling the cork
- ☐ Sticking with the plan
- ☐ Misquoting
- ☐ Forgiving
- ☐ Forgetting
- ☐ Restarting rolls of tape
- ☐ Getting parties started
- ☐ Adapting and overcoming
- ☐ Adapting but not overcoming
- ☐ Hooking up electronic devices
- ☐ Being fearless about trying other people's prescriptions
- ☐ Talking people off ledges (physical)
- ☐ Talking people off ledges (metaphorical)
- ☐ Infusing things with vodka
- ☐ Infusing vodka with things
- ☐ Inserting swear words into regular words
- ☐ Following directions

- [ ] Dwelling on slights
- [ ] Dwelling in a veritable mansion of slights
- [ ] Scraping things clean with your fingernails
- [ ] Estimating if a crowded elevator is over the weight limit
- [ ] Being able to dismiss or exalt cities after having spent a single night in them
- [ ] Knowing which glasses look best on different faces
- [ ] Starting many single-entry blogs
- [ ] Balancing things on the bathtub rim while bathing
- [ ] Using toothpicks attractively
- [ ] Using Q-tips responsibly
- [ ] Folding shirts
- [ ] Wearing pants
- [ ] Remote controlling
- [ ] Cutting your own hair
- [ ] Winning radio contests
- [ ] Not getting upset when your radio contest prizes always consist of two tickets to '70s rock band reunion shows, parking not included
- [ ] Saving the right bric-a-brac
- [ ] Applying reverse psychology
- [ ] Applying double reverse psychology
- [ ] Watching heroin injection scenes without flinching

YOU ARE GOOD AT HIGH SCHOOL COACH THINGS

- [ ] Wielding clipboards
- [ ] Spotting and encouraging hustle
- [ ] Noting and denouncing any lack of hustle
- [ ] Styling sweatsuits
- [ ] Wearing whistles
- [ ] Always knowing how many extra laps are sufficient punishment for different transgressions
- [ ] Knowing when showers need to be hit
- [ ] Using personal tragedies to make stirring halftime speeches
- [ ] Promoting fundamentals
- [ ] Straddling the line between appropriate and inappropriate butt patting
- [ ] Believing deeply in the power of calisthenics to solve real-world problems
- [ ] Sticking with the same haircut
- [ ] Making cuts
- [ ] Humiliating people on the sidelines one day and teaching them government the next
- [ ] Reminding people no one else believes in them
- [ ] Getting everyone's hands in
- [ ] Using the phrase "Tenacious D" appropriately

- ☐ Getting people to reveal how much they make
- ☐ Organizing closets
- ☐ Being cool with closet chaos
- ☐ Knowing state and country capitals
- ☐ Making do
- ☐ Making don't
- ☐ Standing up straight
- ☐ Accepting criticism
- ☐ Scrubbing away shame in the shower
- ☐ Socializing on the mini-golf course
- ☐ Balancing on two chair legs without falling
- ☐ Making dismissive gestures
- ☐ Portioning food out evenly
- ☐ Giving come-hither looks
- ☐ Giving go-up-yonder looks
- ☐ Doing tricks with bottle caps
- ☐ Not freaking out
- ☐ Capturing the moment
- ☐ Setting moments free
- ☐ Wearing earmuffs

- [ ] Adapting to new models
- [ ] Tying shoes and ties on someone else's body
- [ ] Finding buttons that match
- [ ] Cat sitting
- [ ] Shuffling along
- [ ] Knowing when it's acceptable to use the phrase "making love"
- [ ] Snagging the upgrade
- [ ] Announcing that you could make a salad at home for cheaper
- [ ] Reminding people to lift with the legs
- [ ] Giving healing touches
- [ ] Giving touches that don't heal but feel good anyway
- [ ] Accusing people of being divas
- [ ] Noting architectural details
- [ ] Remembering what used to be there
- [ ] Pushing Ma's buttons
- [ ] Figuring out tips
- [ ] Making excuses
- [ ] Saying, "I'm just saying"
- [ ] Always having candy
- [ ] Resisting the urge to eat all the cheese right after grating it

☐ Being the cool older brother

- ☐ Making paper-clip sculptures
- ☐ Bantering at barbecues
- ☐ Remembering where you left off
- ☐ Doing stupid car tricks
- ☐ Having a sixth sense about circuit breaker switches
- ☐ Spotting the Big Dipper
- ☐ Not coming off desperate
- ☐ Solving the Fun Page puzzles
- ☐ Taking deep breaths when appropriate
- ☐ Getting out of the way
- ☐ Standing up to injustice
- ☐ Taking it to the next level
- ☐ Keeping it at the same level
- ☐ Always knowing when postage-stamp-price increases go into effect
- ☐ Applying lotion (to self)
- ☐ Applying lotion (to others)
- ☐ Spotting celebrities
- ☐ Posing for pictures
- ☐ Remembering to take the leftovers
- ☐ Diagramming sentences
- ☐ Not getting caught
- ☐ Mending ways

- [ ] Asking people if you've ever steered them wrong
- [ ] Wiping that smirk off your face
- [ ] Knowing exactly which historical figures you'd have dinner with
- [ ] Seeing things from the other guy's point of view
- [ ] Beating yourself up
- [ ] Sending thank-you notes
- [ ] Winking
- [ ] Starting lawnmowers and snowblowers
- [ ] Making love out of nothing at all
- [ ] Padding résumés
- [ ] Parallel parking
- [ ] Avoiding parallel parking
- [ ] Rising to occasions
- [ ] Maintaining a perfect balance of belief and doubt in horoscopes
- [ ] Customizing jarred spaghetti sauce
- [ ] Embellishing wild-night-out stories
- [ ] Providing feedback
- [ ] Shooting knowing glances
- [ ] Shooting ignorant glances
- [ ] Rerouting cables
- [ ] Spotting hidden cameras
- [ ] Adjusting stereo equalizers

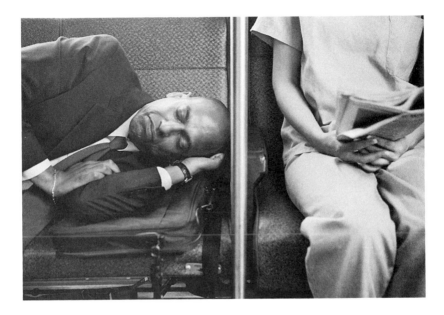

☐ Sleeping on public transportation

- [ ] Keeping score
- [ ] Making pajamas sexy
- [ ] Lurking on the margins
- [ ] Converting regular names into nicknames
- [ ] Getting extensions on due dates
- [ ] Making amends
- [ ] Redirecting feng shui
- [ ] Finagling better seats
- [ ] Managing thermostats
- [ ] Listing pros and cons before making big decisions
- [ ] Ignoring lists of pros and cons before making big decisions
- [ ] Offering condolences
- [ ] Finding "unnecessary" quotation marks funny
- [ ] Letting go
- [ ] Putting things in perspective
- [ ] Borrowing hand trucks
- [ ] Eyeballing acreage
- [ ] Finding cheap flights
- [ ] Bicycling in high style
- [ ] Debunking cherished myths
- [ ] Debunking myths we didn't even realize were cherished until they got debunked

- [ ] Citing precedent
- [ ] Getting keys on and off key rings
- [ ] Blowing straw wrappers across tables
- [ ] Bearing witness
- [ ] Shining your own shoes
- [ ] Wrapping presents using very little tape
- [ ] Taking your own sweet time
- [ ] Remembering the umbrella
- [ ] Guesstimating
- [ ] Flipping the script
- [ ] Taking care to minimize paper towel use
- [ ] Taking care to maximize paper towel use
- [ ] Observing moments of silence
- [ ] Being the one who coughs during a moment of silence
- [ ] Picking the restaurant
- [ ] Picking the movie
- [ ] Sticking up for yourself
- [ ] Tuning radios
- [ ] Coaching people on building fireplace fires
- [ ] Outshining your peers
- [ ] Going down swinging

☐ Promising you'll keep in touch as magical summers come to a close

- ☐ Getting words in edgewise
- ☐ Getting people to move over a seat in theaters
- ☐ Boasting about how bad you are with names
- ☐ Asking people if they think you're a mind reader
- ☐ Keeping up with pen pals
- ☐ Remembering people's birthdays
- ☐ Remembering people's anniversaries
- ☐ Remembering people's allergies
- ☐ Cutting ceremonial ribbons
- ☐ Steering clear
- ☐ Reaching the top shelf
- ☐ Keeping it down
- ☐ Keeping it up
- ☐ Knowing CB lingo
- ☐ Tailgating
- ☐ Having another
- ☐ Eliminating clutter
- ☐ Generating clutter
- ☐ Employing elaborate handshakes
- ☐ Just going with it when someone starts an elaborate handshake with you
- ☐ Righting historical wrongs

- [ ] Blowing up inflatables
- [ ] Crafting study-hall origami
- [ ] Liking jellybean flavors nobody else likes
- [ ] Not asking questions
- [ ] Asking questions later
- [ ] Refusing to be put on hold
- [ ] Picking the fastest line
- [ ] Picking the fastest lane
- [ ] Reminding yourself that all the lanes and lines are about the same
- [ ] Picking up the spare
- [ ] Not calling it a comeback
- [ ] Remaining expressionless while the court renders its verdict
- [ ] Adding, "When you get a chance . . ."
- [ ] Working the phrase "I'm not going to tell you how to do your job" into discussions where you tell people how to do their job
- [ ] Comparing things to summer rain
- [ ] Making photo albums
- [ ] Being a "man on the street"
- [ ] Maintaining a diary
- [ ] Resort livin'
- [ ] Having an appropriately apologetic expression when paying with dollar coins

☐ Putting dishes away in other people's kitchens

YOU ARE GOOD AT ATTENDING WEDDING THINGS

- [ ] Helping the best man turn three bawdy anecdotes into a touching speech
- [ ] Seeing that flower petals get tossed instead of rice
- [ ] Sending in RSVP cards quickly
- [ ] Knowing when the table centerpieces are free for the taking
- [ ] Being a stickler about not "congratulating" the bride
- [ ] Picking the best, and best-priced, stuff off the gift registry
- [ ] Having a sixth sense about which entrée to choose
- [ ] Promoting conviviality on the bus to the venue
- [ ] Understanding the traffic flow of passed hors d'oeuvres and positioning yourself accordingly
- [ ] Ratcheting up enthusiasm on the dance floor
- [ ] Ratcheting down enthusiasm on the dance floor

- [ ] Advising people on what they can and can't get away with when the invitation says "black tie"
- [ ] Conversing with the officiant
- [ ] Helping bridesmaids feel better about the dresses they've been forced to wear

- ☐ Reading lips
- ☐ Making introductions
- ☐ Breaking into a jog
- ☐ Going sockless
- ☐ Revving engines
- ☐ Wiping your feet
- ☐ Convincing the shopkeeper to open back up, even though they just closed for the night
- ☐ Extracting confessions
- ☐ Chewing thoroughly
- ☐ Going to the woods to live deliberately
- ☐ Going to the woods to live obliviously
- ☐ Inventing road trip games
- ☐ Relaxing on the porch
- ☐ Kicking back on the stoop
- ☐ Chilling in the gas station parking lot
- ☐ Citing actuarial statistics
- ☐ Feigning indifference
- ☐ Celebrating difference
- ☐ Staining glass
- ☐ Blowing glass
- ☐ Walking on broken glass
- ☐ Making radish roses

- [ ] Making people feel guilty
- [ ] Having and showing off the latest gadgetry
- [ ] Illustrating chalkboard menus
- [ ] Establishing causality
- [ ] Planning events
- [ ] Following the sun
- [ ] Being like the lilies of the field
- [ ] Snipping the lilies of the field and putting them in a vase to help brighten a room
- [ ] Considering alternatives
- [ ] Admitting you have a problem
- [ ] Battling inner demons
- [ ] Making inner demons feel at home
- [ ] Knowing thyself
- [ ] Stenciling
- [ ] Feeling the pain of everyone
- [ ] Seeing the big picture
- [ ] Knowing where fans should be placed for maximum cooling
- [ ] Snuffing candles with your fingertips
- [ ] Dancing so people want to imitate you
- [ ] Pillow talking
- [ ] Walking it off

- ☐ Embracing new synonyms for the human buttocks
- ☐ Drawing up good sandlot football plays on your palm
- ☐ Living with regret
- ☐ Sticking it to the man
- ☐ Getting stuck by the man
- ☐ Playing footsie
- ☐ Suspecting dinner companions of playing footsie
- ☐ Giving beggars advice on shelters rather than cash
- ☐ Serenely accepting whatever happens
- ☐ Beer-battering
- ☐ Bottling it all up inside
- ☐ Horsing around
- ☐ Misinterpreting dreams
- ☐ Formulating plans for revitalizing the downtown
- ☐ Sectioning grapefruit
- ☐ Rolling your own
- ☐ Collecting all four
- ☐ Connecting all four
- ☐ Being a regular
- ☐ Packing light
- ☐ Being a poet without even knowing it
- ☐ Clearing the air
- ☐ Sweating to oldies

- [ ] Following up
- [ ] Bedazzling
- [ ] Citing rules about when you should wear white
- [ ] Transferring files
- [ ] Naming that tune
- [ ] Learning only from the History Channel
- [ ] Putting a dollar value on that which is beyond price
- [ ] Not accepting Sprite when you asked for 7UP
- [ ] Packing the cooler
- [ ] Spending gift cards in a timely and practical fashion
- [ ] Bellying up to the bar
- [ ] Lighting up a room
- [ ] Righting kayaks
- [ ] Fitting into old jeans
- [ ] Harassing ballplayers
- [ ] Tagging along
- [ ] Picking people up at the airport
- [ ] Converting nonbelievers
- [ ] Threatening to move to Canada
- [ ] Letting people stay with you for longer than they should
- [ ] Curtsying

☐ Being a good first date

- [ ] Not taking offense
- [ ] Making full use of the season pass
- [ ] Seizing the day
- [ ] Interrogating the day
- [ ] Beating the day in such a way that you don't leave any suspicious marks
- [ ] Climbing wobbly ladders
- [ ] Pitching softballs into rigged bushel baskets
- [ ] Shooting out stars completely
- [ ] Spraying water into the mouths of plastic clowns
- [ ] Supporting local businesses
- [ ] Waxing nostalgic
- [ ] Watching squirrels
- [ ] Hugging it out
- [ ] Using industry lingo of industries you're not a part of
- [ ] Making that old guitar sing
- [ ] Threading needles
- [ ] Threadin' the needle
- [ ] Not asking "Do I really sound like that?" when hearing your recorded voice
- [ ] Pointing out when a responsibility isn't your department
- [ ] Noting how this time it's personal
- [ ] Considerately noting when regrettable transactions are business rather than personal

- ☐ Bowing down to no man
- ☐ Acting like wherever you are is the place to be
- ☐ Getting impulse tattoos
- ☐ Publicly displaying affection
- ☐ Messing around with gender roles
- ☐ Looking like you mean business
- ☐ Not letting it get to you
- ☐ Shredding (cheese)
- ☐ Shredding (guitar)
- ☐ Shredding (sensitive documents)
- ☐ Shredding (snowboard)
- ☐ Asking if there's anything you can do to help and meaning it
- ☐ Reading over people's shoulders
- ☐ Not minding when people read over your shoulders
- ☐ Reconciling yourself to loss
- ☐ Playing drinking games
- ☐ Convincing otherwise reasonable people to play drinking games
- ☐ Making us believe again
- ☐ Defying calls for your resignation
- ☐ Finding genuinely witty bumper stickers and aprons
- ☐ Threateningly asking people if they're looking at you

☐ Getting out and stretching

- ☐ Not letting executive washroom privileges go to your head
- ☐ Treating others as you wish to be treated
- ☐ Going rogue
- ☐ Skipping right to the dirty part
- ☐ Reading bus schedules
- ☐ Listening for the buzzer
- ☐ Letting people know when they've just made a powerful enemy
- ☐ Not getting your water glass all fingerprinty
- ☐ Bar brawling
- ☐ Waiting for pizza to cool before eating it
- ☐ Sticking landings
- ☐ Seeing it coming
- ☐ Catching stacks of coins flipped off your arms
- ☐ Waiting and getting it on sale
- ☐ Putting things back where you found them
- ☐ Cobbling together a makeshift faith
- ☐ Financing things
- ☐ Refinancing things
- ☐ Assembling slideshows
- ☐ Picking music for slideshows
- ☐ Sizing up competition

- [ ] Spotting all the differences between two similar pictures
- [ ] Being able to tell the difference between drums and a drum machine
- [ ] Riding the rails
- [ ] Blowing rails
- [ ] Railing against the status quo
- [ ] Noting when it's good sleeping weather
- [ ] Looking busy in airports
- [ ] Wearing glasses on top of your head
- [ ] Extending courtesies
- [ ] Lording it over others
- [ ] Not lording it over others
- [ ] Pogo sticking
- [ ] Picking out fabric
- [ ] Amassing honorary degrees
- [ ] Asking doctors to give it to you straight
- [ ] Getting out of noncompete clauses
- [ ] Balancing checkbooks
- [ ] Not staring
- [ ] Calling foot faults during casual games
- [ ] Not going nuts when opponents call foot faults in casual games
- [ ] Knowing just how aggressively to play shuffleboard or croquet without coming off as a jerk

☐ Staying calm when you accidentally take home the wrong suitcase

- ☐ Placing accents
- ☐ Not shaking hands when you're sick
- ☐ Waking up without an alarm
- ☐ Answering your own questions
- ☐ Showing restraint
- ☐ Possessing restraint, but not showing it
- ☐ Freestyling
- ☐ Freewheeling
- ☐ Jazzercising
- ☐ Layering
- ☐ Opening bags of chips without spilling them all over
- ☐ Fearlessly sitting in the front row
- ☐ Asking people to do the math
- ☐ Doubling down
- ☐ Reforming bad boys
- ☐ Being a bad boy
- ☐ Loving bad boys just as they are
- ☐ Playing mind games
- ☐ Not knowing how to define important things, but knowing them when you see them
- ☐ Being as good as your word
- ☐ Slacking

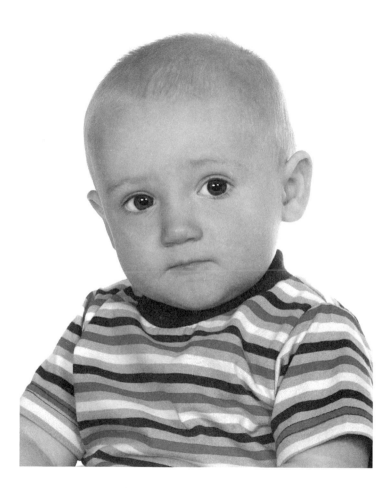

☐ Having the appearance of thinking wise thoughts

- [ ] Running to catch planes and trains
- [ ] Getting the ball in the cup
- [ ] Getting animals to swallow pills
- [ ] Popping wheelies
- [ ] Popping and locking
- [ ] Popping in unexpectedly
- [ ] Spotting designer knockoffs
- [ ] Dishing it out
- [ ] Taking it
- [ ] Crossing your legs in a way that defies gender expectations
- [ ] Maximizing battery life
- [ ] Changing filters regularly
- [ ] Making innocent things sound dirty
- [ ] Apologizing on behalf of others
- [ ] Picking out ties
- [ ] Dressing dogs
- [ ] Being Up to Speed on All the Latest Acronyms (BUTSO-ATLA)
- [ ] Inventing new acronyms
- [ ] Adding witty rejoinders
- [ ] Adding rejoinders that aren't so witty, but'll do
- [ ] Diagnosing people without knowing or examining them, while possessing no medical credentials or training

☐ Applying what you've learned from mobster shows and
movies to real life

- [ ] Mediating disputes
- [ ] Making flashcards
- [ ] Always hitting the after-party
- [ ] Finding hidden Masonic imagery
- [ ] Not hitting "Reply All"
- [ ] Carving turkeys
- [ ] Asking them to turn it down
- [ ] Making jeans into cutoffs
- [ ] Knowing how to unlock the hallucinogenic properties of common household goods
- [ ] Making it look like an accident
- [ ] Whittling
- [ ] Sending in warranty cards
- [ ] Suffering in silence
- [ ] Knowing your hat and ring size
- [ ] Knowing the hat and ring size of your significant other
- [ ] Letting them know you've been there
- [ ] Acting like you own the joint
- [ ] Not letting them get you down
- [ ] Being able to tell the difference between bug bites and zits
- [ ] Microwaving burritos evenly
- [ ] Tracing things back to their source
- [ ] Sending mixed signals

☐ Visiting your old teachers

- [ ] Lying to yourself
- [ ] Blending into foreign cultures
- [ ] Forging signatures
- [ ] Forging ahead
- [ ] Wreaking a terrible vengeance
- [ ] Bringing enough to share with everyone
- [ ] Getting combatants to shake and make up
- [ ] Integrating disparate elements into one harmonious whole
- [ ] Knitting in public
- [ ] Threatening to take your name off projects
- [ ] Staring out of train windows, pondering
- [ ] Bodysurfing
- [ ] Determining PSI in tires and basketballs by feel
- [ ] Figuring how far away lightning is by counting out thunder
- [ ] Getting hoisted with your own petard
- [ ] Hoisting others by their petards
- [ ] Non-petard-related hoisting
- [ ] Fulfilling prophesies
- [ ] Turning the beat around
- [ ] Tying trench coat belts with conviction and flair
- [ ] Finding substitute ingredients
- [ ] Popularizing arcane causes

- ☐ Rolling your eyes
- ☐ Rolling with your posse
- ☐ Rolling sushi
- ☐ Rolling bones
- ☐ Coming in for the kill
- ☐ Frequently and drastically revising your will
- ☐ Buying rounds
- ☐ Supporting your local music scene
- ☐ Combining sodas at the 7-Eleven to create viable "new" sodas
- ☐ Treating old people with respect, if not reverence
- ☐ Clipping things to your belt
- ☐ Obeying your sensei without question
- ☐ Living and learning
- ☐ Living without learning
- ☐ Finding and exploiting tax loopholes
- ☐ Making contingency plans
- ☐ Enforcing old codes of etiquette
- ☐ Scooping the loop
- ☐ Getting lost in the clouds
- ☐ Hiding signs of intoxication from authority figures
- ☐ Redistributing wealth
- ☐ Maxing out at breakfast buffets
- ☐ Finger painting

YOU ARE GOOD AT BRAINY THINGS

You don't need no stinking reference book!

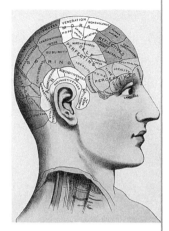

You already know:

- ☐ The order of poker hands
- ☐ Boxing weight classes
- ☐ The track and field events
- ☐ The deadly sins
- ☐ The major acting techniques
- ☐ The official names for all the pasta shapes
- ☐ Correlations between European and American shoe sizes (not just your own)
- ☐ The dates and reputed personality traits of all the zodiac signs (not just your own)
- ☐ Which leaves go with which trees
- ☐ What colors go with which gangs
- ☐ The succession of presidents at the major TV networks
- ☐ The hierarchy in the Church
- ☐ The hierarchy of military ranks
- ☐ The official phonetic alphabet (alpha, bravo . . .)
- ☐ The cuts of meat
- ☐ The sex symbols of previous generations
- ☐ The three-letter codes of the major airports

- [ ] Philosophizing
- [ ] Memorizing license plate numbers
- [ ] Being a vegetarian with exceptions
- [ ] Splurging
- [ ] Treating yourself
- [ ] Noting whenever people have really let themselves go
- [ ] Knowing just what letters to ink onto your knuckles
- [ ] Stoking ancient tribal enmities
- [ ] Finding new uses for old toothbrushes
- [ ] Blurring the line between navy and black
- [ ] Not holding things against people
- [ ] Basking
- [ ] Boldly taking library books to the beach
- [ ] Living in the shadows
- [ ] Reaching troubled campers
- [ ] Straightening plants with sticks
- [ ] Pruning bonsais
- [ ] Staying best friends with your exes
- [ ] Knowing what things are exclusively "for chumps" and declaring them so
- [ ] Taking one for the team
- [ ] Seeing the wonder of all creation in a single blade of grass

- ☐ Upselling
- ☐ Trapping tourists
- ☐ Keeping things aboveboard
- ☐ Conferring
- ☐ Returning purchases
- ☐ Pulling pranks
- ☐ Knowing when a prank has gone too far
- ☐ Having no shame
- ☐ Having some shame
- ☐ Describing car trouble sounds so the mechanic understands
- ☐ Postponing your dissertation
- ☐ Inventing new abbreviations (abbrevs)
- ☐ Adjusting hydraulic office chairs
- ☐ Going door to door
- ☐ Presenting a unified front
- ☐ Snazzily repairing torn folders
- ☐ Knowing alphabetical order without having to recite the alphabet
- ☐ Being a master of the batting cage
- ☐ Being a master of the driving range
- ☐ Hiding your true feelings
- ☐ Highlighting important passages
- ☐ Learning languages from science-fiction shows

☐ Keeping detailed records of gambling losses for tax purposes

- ☐ Power lunching
- ☐ Spotting fake IDs
- ☐ Inquiring within
- ☐ Determining if letters weigh more or less than 1 ounce without using a scale
- ☐ Exhibiting all the classic symptoms
- ☐ Flinging open French doors
- ☐ Remembering to pick up the dry cleaning
- ☐ Explaining yourself
- ☐ Letting establishments know that their soap dispenser is empty
- ☐ Acting like it's no big deal
- ☐ Rounding up suspects
- ☐ Teaching chain stores a lesson by not shopping at them for a while
- ☐ Yanking chains
- ☐ Feeling the burn
- ☐ Bending spoons using only the power of your mind
- ☐ Identifying new species
- ☐ Telling strangers when they've dropped something
- ☐ Rocking the boat
- ☐ Rocking the vote
- ☐ Continuing to rock in the free world
- ☐ Imitating Rocky

- ☐ Not fainting at the sight of blood
- ☐ Getting tickets ahead of time
- ☐ Walking expectantly across vast plazas
- ☐ Saving seats
- ☐ Pulling the old switcheroo
- ☐ Picking out ripe melons
- ☐ Carefully labeling the giant foil-wrapped packages in the freezer
- ☐ Recruiting ringers
- ☐ Riding double
- ☐ Knowing when to keep your mouth shut
- ☐ Imagining heretofore unimagined sushi roll combos
- ☐ Knowing when and where dirty jokes are appropriate
- ☐ Forgetting punch lines
- ☐ Making perfume samples last
- ☐ Remembering your epinephrine injector
- ☐ Tending window box gardens
- ☐ Finding secret places in the library to make out in
- ☐ Developing various impressive things that are already within you
- ☐ Defending Israel
- ☐ Criticizing Israel
- ☐ Ignoring Israel
- ☐ Acting all big

- ☐ Pointing out false dichotomies
- ☐ Pointing out true dichotomies
- ☐ Lolling about in a daze
- ☐ Making wastepaper-basket baskets
- ☐ Disrespecting people without meaning any disrespect
- ☐ Calling meetings to order
- ☐ Having especially valuable body parts insured
- ☐ Organizing surprise parties
- ☐ Memorizing lines
- ☐ Skipping grades
- ☐ Dancing in place
- ☐ Conducting midnight raids
- ☐ Finding housesitting gigs
- ☐ Repelling others from sitting next to you on buses and trains
- ☐ Remembering dreams
- ☐ Inducing vomiting
- ☐ Knowing whether you're supposed to induce vomiting or drink milk
- ☐ Pulling all-nighters
- ☐ Having a little faith
- ☐ Finding the car in parking garages and endless lots
- ☐ Making bail
- ☐ Creating best-of lists at the end of each year

☐ Refusing to acknowledge that the shortcut has gotten you lost

- [ ] Hiding out
- [ ] Sneaking into construction sites
- [ ] Peeking into construction sites
- [ ] Wondering what it's all for
- [ ] Comparing bands to other bands
- [ ] Setting the mood
- [ ] Letting backyard swing sets decay majestically
- [ ] Neatly folding paper bags
- [ ] Overestimating your ability to handle spicy foods
- [ ] Driving go-karts to win
- [ ] Rescuing earthworms
- [ ] Smooth-talking nightclub bouncers
- [ ] Making yourself useful
- [ ] Tearing ads out of magazines
- [ ] Pulling tablecloths off set tables without spilling anything
- [ ] Stacking creamers
- [ ] Being consistent with what words you misspell
- [ ] Riffing
- [ ] Backtracking
- [ ] Protesting
- [ ] Making fun of protesters
- [ ] Having appropriate facial expressions when passing groups of protesters (e.g., one that says, "I sympathize with your cause, but not enough to join you—sorry")

- [ ] Fighting for your right to party
- [ ] Graciously ceding your right to party
- [ ] Deciphering cryptic restroom signage
- [ ] Being aware of racist roots of common terms
- [ ] Catching flies with eating utensils
- [ ] Guessing secret knocks
- [ ] Discovering great new writers
- [ ] Expecting calls
- [ ] Just messin' with people
- [ ] Calling time out
- [ ] Tuning out the noise
- [ ] Using shoe trees
- [ ] Starting over
- [ ] Untangling cords
- [ ] Letting sandals dangle
- [ ] Having smart things to say about art
- [ ] Having smart-sounding things to say about art
- [ ] Dealing with the household help in a respectful, not-condescending way
- [ ] Getting good gifts for people at airports
- [ ] Getting good gifts for people before you get to the airport

- [ ] Grifting
- [ ] Announcing how drunk or high you are
- [ ] Sharing zucchini with the neighbors
- [ ] Knowing what to do in emergencies
- [ ] Actually doing the right thing in emergencies
- [ ] Keeping lots of plates spinning (metaphorically)
- [ ] Keeping lots of plates spinning (literally)
- [ ] Getting the student discount even though you've been out of school for years
- [ ] Offering guests something to drink right away
- [ ] Finding new groups to pal around with
- [ ] Flipping the mattress regularly
- [ ] Overdiagnosing yourself
- [ ] Hearing cell phones vibrate from far away
- [ ] Bringing macho to the diaper bag
- [ ] Assigning people a numerical rating based on their physical attractiveness
- [ ] Arranging swaps
- [ ] Going solo
- [ ] Plucking invisible hairs from your shirt
- [ ] Saving up for a rainy day
- [ ] Going on rainy-day sprees
- [ ] Catching whatever it is that's going around

☐ Subtly flashing your wad of bills

- ☐ Scaring away all the customers
- ☐ Always having the same o'clock shadow
- ☐ Knowing who's had work done
- ☐ Taking the stairs two at a time
- ☐ Taking the stairs three at a time
- ☐ Taking the stairs four at a time!
- ☐ Untangling kite string
- ☐ Executing the perfect s'more
- ☐ Knowing all the words to fight songs
- ☐ Not letting your not knowing the words to fight songs slow you down
- ☐ Knowing song lyric origin stories
- ☐ Pretending you didn't just see that
- ☐ Being meek
- ☐ Inheriting the earth
- ☐ Always knowing the date
- ☐ Squeezing out appropriately coin-sized amounts of liquids
- ☐ Advocating for world peace on T-shirts
- ☐ Advocating for whirled peas on T-shirts
- ☐ Stealing newspapers
- ☐ Worshipping false idols

- ☐ Pointing out tiny unrealistic details in movies ("That cloned alien cyborg would never wear those socks!")
- ☐ Honoring your mother and father
- ☐ Blaming MTV
- ☐ Remembering not to rub your eyes or genitals after handling hot peppers
- ☐ Making deathbed speeches
- ☐ Getting everything important said pre-deathbed
- ☐ Remembering to log out
- ☐ Playing crabgrass kazoos
- ☐ Knowing which snakes are harmless
- ☐ Getting bumper cars out of jams
- ☐ Looking but not really seeing
- ☐ Conspiracy theorizing
- ☐ Forming dreadlocks
- ☐ Rotating halfway through baking
- ☐ Pointing out what does and doesn't grow on trees
- ☐ Sending emails with time stamps that make people ask, "When is it you sleep exactly?"
- ☐ Quickly spotting the part of the sidewalk that caused you to trip
- ☐ Keeping content on your hard drive that is still able to shock snooping computer-repair people

☐ Dressing appropriately for hikes in the forest

- ☐ Hocking loogies
- ☐ Photobombing
- ☐ Doubling back
- ☐ Knowing when a style has moved from stale to vintage
- ☐ Inventing euphemisms for firing people
- ☐ Using euphemisms for firing people
- ☐ Adhering to every grammar rule learned in grammar school
- ☐ Laying it on pretty thick
- ☐ Inspiring people in ways you can't even imagine
- ☐ Helpfully pointing out when there ain't no stopping you
- ☐ Not being afraid to ask whether those are real
- ☐ Coming up with fresh prom themes
- ☐ Being thorough with drop-cloth placement when painting
- ☐ Not wasting any more time
- ☐ Assembling crack squadrons
- ☐ Assembling regular squadrons
- ☐ Speculating on who is and isn't mobbed up
- ☐ Granting leniency
- ☐ Reigning in blood
- ☐ Reigning in bodily fluids other than blood
- ☐ Being able to expound for hours on the difference between geeks and nerds

☐ Staging family portraits that are *just* normal enough not
   to be featured on websites that mock and celebrate goofy
   family portraits

- [ ] Dancing away the heartache
- [ ] Playing the percentages
- [ ] Being self-actualized
- [ ] Being okay with not being self-actualized
- [ ] Saying, "I don't want to jinx it, but…"
- [ ] Knowing when a bullet has your name on it
- [ ] Sleeping in
- [ ] Knowing when places open
- [ ] Knowing when places close
- [ ] Commuting
- [ ] Comprehending the voice coming over the box at the fast-food drive-thru
- [ ] Being the Monopoly banker
- [ ] Counting calories
- [ ] Discounting calories
- [ ] Extruding things
- [ ] Repurposing hearses
- [ ] Saying no
- [ ] Saying, "NOOOOOO!"
- [ ] Giving kids names that will never appear on key chains at gift shops
- [ ] Eating ice pops non-suggestively
- [ ] Being aware of movie-release dates

☐ Knowing when a window air-conditioning unit is "secure enough"

- [ ] Politely declining offers
- [ ] Knowing which companies did business with the Nazis
- [ ] Coming up with good DJ names
- [ ] Being aware of who drew first blood
- [ ] Bicycling and not being righteous about it
- [ ] Being excited when old houses have dumbwaiters
- [ ] Trying again later
- [ ] Getting free trial memberships to the gym
- [ ] Having your goofy British, Irish, and Scottish accent imitations be noticeably different
- [ ] Correctly guessing the attendance at sporting events
- [ ] Keeping your age secret
- [ ] Keeping your weight secret
- [ ] Keeping your SAT scores secret
- [ ] Rearranging hotel room furniture
- [ ] Interacting with babies
- [ ] Always knowing how much cash is in your wallet
- [ ] Predicting the next gumball color
- [ ] Jotting things down
- [ ] Playing for keeps
- [ ] Requesting additional funds

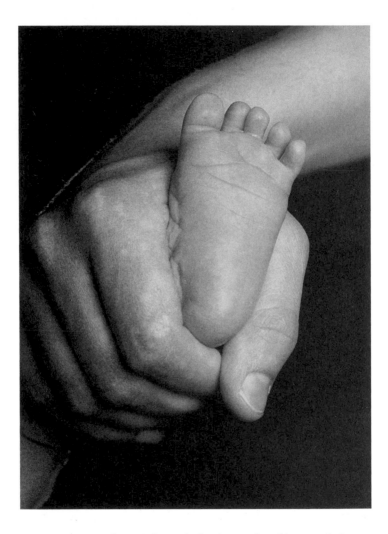

☐ Forcing people to acknowledge how adorable your baby's foot is

- [ ] Picking a slow-dance style in junior high and sticking with it forever
- [ ] Referring to your family by its name
- [ ] Demanding to talk to supervisors
- [ ] Canceling subscriptions
- [ ] Lecturing the young about gathering sexual rosebuds
- [ ] Ruminating
- [ ] Noticing ceilings
- [ ] Being embarrassed on behalf of others
- [ ] Resisting the urge to buy in bulk
- [ ] Rotating stock
- [ ] Unjamming drawers
- [ ] Convincing everyone to play charades
- [ ] Playing charades
- [ ] Writing things on windows in soap
- [ ] Moving on
- [ ] Acting like you don't have a care in the world
- [ ] Acting like you have every care in the world
- [ ] Being swept up in the zeitgeist
- [ ] Steering clear of the zeitgeist
- [ ] Keeping it old school
- [ ] Sweeping for bugs
- [ ] Mixing kiddie cocktails

YOU ARE GOOD AT COLLEGE ENGLISH TEACHER THINGS

☐ Flouting copyright laws

☐ Belittling colleagues' reading lists

☐ Showing movies whenever possible and referring to them as "filmic texts"

☐ Emphasizing process over product

☐ Being on a first-name basis with students

☐ Only dealing with the alternative bookstore

☐ Forcing students to attend plays and readings

☐ Openly insulting the administration

☐ Being the default teacher-crush

☐ Employing slightly stale pop culture references to help make literature relevant

☐ Giving B-minuses when you should be giving C-minuses

☐ Blaming email and text messaging for debasing language skills

☐ Adamantly leaving the chairs in a circle when class is over

☐ Teaching from the desk

- ☐ Predicting reality show victors
- ☐ Using all the cool "hit me" gestures in blackjack
- ☐ Not blinking first
- ☐ Cartwheeling
- ☐ Keeping it together
- ☐ Blowing it apart
- ☐ Saying "You're welcome" to prompt a "Thank you"
- ☐ Breast-feeding modestly in public
- ☐ Walking great distances in flip-flops
- ☐ Bringing plants back from the brink
- ☐ Getting excited when places declare themselves to be under new management
- ☐ Dumbing it down
- ☐ Blowing bubbles
- ☐ Blowing bubbles within bubbles
- ☐ Growing herbs
- ☐ Picking horses
- ☐ Crunching gravel
- ☐ Crunching numbers
- ☐ Doing something unusual for a year and writing a memoir about it
- ☐ Doing something unusual for longer than a year and not writing a memoir about it
- ☐ Remembering to bring the reusable bag to the grocery store

☐ Picking jukebox songs that everyone in the room agrees with

- [ ] Leaving critical notes on windshields
- [ ] Knowing when you're not wanted
- [ ] Being a contender
- [ ] Being aware of the fact that you could've been a contender
- [ ] Knowing when bribes are appropriate
- [ ] Cleaning apples on your shirt
- [ ] Working the phrase "This is where the magic happens" into house tours
- [ ] Continuing to bemoan the commodification of cool
- [ ] Lambasting youth fashion trends
- [ ] Seeing the wit and beauty of youth fashion trends
- [ ] Exploiting youth fashion trends for money
- [ ] Urging school-district-wide bans on youth fashion trends
- [ ] Finding places to hang a garment bag in a pinch
- [ ] Scraping gum off shoes
- [ ] Fighting the power
- [ ] Letting the power have its way with you
- [ ] Vacuuming under the floor mats
- [ ] Asking people if they need a lift
- [ ] Spotting wedding rings
- [ ] Starting the wave
- [ ] Stifling sneezes
- [ ] Confronting litterbugs

- ☐ Maintaining control at self-serve ice cream stations
- ☐ Building suspense
- ☐ Talking about difficult topics with kids
- ☐ Holding your palm over candles
- ☐ Knowing just the right amount of French and Latin
- ☐ Using folk stain-removal methods
- ☐ Making "son of a bitch" a term of endearment
- ☐ Rolling up your sleeves
- ☐ Embracing every Internet fad
- ☐ Protecting babies from sunshine
- ☐ Fending off snack attacks
- ☐ Remembering the gym locker combo even when you rarely make it to the gym
- ☐ Staying gold
- ☐ Judging wind direction and speed with only a licked finger
- ☐ Knowing the right music to blast from your car stereo
- ☐ Sharpening pencils evenly
- ☐ Knowing when to upgrade coworkers to colleagues
- ☐ Wearing suspenders
- ☐ Making quadruple-decker peanut butter sandwiches
- ☐ Figuring when the Christmas lights have been up long enough that you might as well leave them up
- ☐ Keeping a cheese diary

☐ Navigating the information superhighway

- ☐ Using coin-op shoe polishers whenever you get the chance
- ☐ Doing things in bed without waking the person next to you
- ☐ Recognizing taillights
- ☐ Using the bike bell
- ☐ Completely removing unwanted whipped cream from hot drinks with a straw
- ☐ Announcing whenever the hunter has become the hunted
- ☐ Announcing whenever the student has become the master
- ☐ Knowing how to work the shower in unfamiliar bathrooms
- ☐ Sucking an entire mint without chewing or cracking it
- ☐ Planting beach umbrellas
- ☐ Organizing bags in car trunks
- ☐ Cleanly twisting ice out of trays
- ☐ Adjusting and folding aluminum lounge chairs
- ☐ Using colorful terms for vomiting
- ☐ Doing push-ups in unusual places
- ☐ Laughing easily
- ☐ Stopping stopwatches at exactly .00
- ☐ Using played-out catchphrases in ways that feel fresh
- ☐ Carving out time to nap
- ☐ Treating children like adults
- ☐ Overcoming adversity

- [ ] Yelling "Heads up!" when appropriate
- [ ] Instinctively knowing when a "heads-up!" yelled in the vicinity applies to you
- [ ] Taking eager advantage of new beer-drinking technologies
- [ ] Knowing the difference between a beer belly and a potbelly
- [ ] Finding new tights in an emergency
- [ ] Knowing the appropriate level of participation and enthusiasm when at a worship service not of your religion
- [ ] Doing biceps curls with grocery bags
- [ ] Knowing when retail therapy is more cost-effective than regular therapy
- [ ] Always having a go-to fix-it guy
- [ ] Having a life that is driven by things other than purpose
- [ ] Signing documents on people's backs
- [ ] Spotting undercover cop cars
- [ ] Driving the point home
- [ ] Driving the point along some twisting road, dropping it off in the woods, and letting it fend for itself
- [ ] Holding on to the bottle until you get to a recycling bin
- [ ] Keeping your middle name under wraps
- [ ] Not getting separated from the group
- [ ] Laughing at yourself
- [ ] Laughing at others
- [ ] Always using the more difficult word

☐ Having very specific ideas about how you like your tea

- [ ] Toting a squash racket
- [ ] Toting a yoga mat
- [ ] Letting people know that hammering the elevator button won't make it work any faster
- [ ] Following the careers of Olympians after the Olympics
- [ ] Coming up with counterexamples
- [ ] Getting involved in street-level disputes that have nothing to do with you
- [ ] Giving props to your peeps
- [ ] Withholding props from your peeps
- [ ] Paying your respects
- [ ] Keeping birthday wishes plausible
- [ ] Having a preternatural sense of which side is up with USB plugs
- [ ] Whistling "Dixie"
- [ ] Whistling "Taxi"
- [ ] Calling violas "fiddles"
- [ ] Making stalking funny again
- [ ] Deleting unused apps
- [ ] Always being the first one in the car to call a house with an unkempt yard a crack house
- [ ] Not complaining about mosquitoes unless they're *really* bad
- [ ] Getting excited about dragonflies
- [ ] Eating the turkey leg
- [ ] Carrying emery boards, even though you're male

- [ ] Threatening to make citizen's arrests
- [ ] Actually making citizen's arrests
- [ ] Taking yawns personally
- [ ] Reshelving books correctly
- [ ] Applying toothpaste so it looks like it does in the commercials
- [ ] Applying condiments so they look like they do in the commercials
- [ ] Labeling things
- [ ] Ladling things
- [ ] Adjusting shoulder straps to the ideal length
- [ ] Knowing the odds, when you like them, and saying so
- [ ] Protecting your belongings while sleeping in the park
- [ ] Not falling for the obvious but incorrect answer on optical illusion puzzles
- [ ] Thoroughly reading lengthy online contracts before clicking "Agree"
- [ ] Going all-out for Earth Day
- [ ] Keeping a tea drawer that awes guests
- [ ] Knowing when beautiful should be spelled or pronounced "bee-yoo-tee-ful!"
- [ ] Letting ice cream soften before scooping it
- [ ] Syncing your calendars
- [ ] Letting strangers know when they're raising their kids wrong

☐ Popping lenses back in

- ☐ Coaching drivers through tricky highway exits
- ☐ Creating and sustaining an anonymous online commenter persona
- ☐ Deciphering letters traced on your back
- ☐ Being aware which plants among us are poisonous
- ☐ Following through on threats to write a children's book
- ☐ Talking about how much you like people-watching
- ☐ Knowing the difference between May-December couples and father-daughter pairings
- ☐ Seizing monogramming opportunities
- ☐ Picking up extra credits during the summer session
- ☐ Picking on people your own size
- ☐ Living in stereo
- ☐ Asking strangers where they got their shoes
- ☐ Lacing shoes creatively
- ☐ Lacing shoes like it's the early 1980s
- ☐ Resembling *The Thinker* while thinking
- ☐ Using dollar signs instead of plain old *S*'s
- ☐ Solving fictional crimes
- ☐ Pursuing fleeting fun at the cost of lasting pain
- ☐ Storing extra buttons in one place
- ☐ Maintaining a youthful sense of wonder
- ☐ Keeping it real
- ☐ Announcing whenever you're keeping it real

- ☐ Checking out their other locations
- ☐ Riding three abreast
- ☐ Getting your deposit back
- ☐ Taking off at intermission
- ☐ Living the dream
- ☐ Getting an eyeful
- ☐ Catching an earful
- ☐ Using examples to support your arguments
- ☐ Appreciating what you have
- ☐ Appreciating what others have
- ☐ Assuming it'll all be online
- ☐ Carrying dogs
- ☐ Forgiving Ma for throwing out your old concert T-shirts
- ☐ Differentiating between wavy and curly hair
- ☐ Making exaggerated sounds of relief while urinating
- ☐ Pulling fast ones
- ☐ Working in a quick set of dips
- ☐ Arranging lunch dates
- ☐ Seeing political, environmental, or sporting events as signs of the apocalypse
- ☐ Being realistic about how much the reacquisition of an old childhood toy can really take you back
- ☐ Making a break for it
- ☐ Being there when it counts

☐ Taking up skiing solely for the cozy lodges and sweaters

- ☐ Knowing what you want to order right away
- ☐ Tending community gardens
- ☐ Anonymously reporting unsafe conditions
- ☐ Reading historical plaques out loud
- ☐ Noting which foundry made various sewer grates and manhole covers
- ☐ Showing an interest
- ☐ Wondering where all the time went
- ☐ Knowing damn well where all the time went
- ☐ Dispensing vigilante justice
- ☐ Faking it till you make it
- ☐ Faking it without making it
- ☐ Wearing shoes that clomp authoritatively
- ☐ Taking in wounded animals
- ☐ Thinking people are looking at you through their sunglasses
- ☐ Feeling the electricity
- ☐ Sizing up situations
- ☐ Managing to slap people in the backseat while driving
- ☐ Using all available pockets
- ☐ Checking the brands of people's neckties
- ☐ Organizing picnic games

- ☐ Being the person in line who people ask what the line is for
- ☐ Noticing pedicures
- ☐ Neutralizing threats
- ☐ Leaving in a huff
- ☐ Taking great pride in passport stamps
- ☐ Knowing which Galleria is being referred to
- ☐ Being confident about who you were in a past life
- ☐ Being confident about who you'll be in a future life
- ☐ Being confident about who you are in this life
- ☐ Finding quality walking sticks
- ☐ Asking people if that book is any good
- ☐ Waiting until it comes on cable
- ☐ Doodling three-dimensional cubes
- ☐ Writing things on people's faces while they sleep
- ☐ Being secretly relieved
- ☐ Making trenchant observations
- ☐ Quickly deciphering complex parking regulation signs
- ☐ Carrying five things at once
- ☐ Getting places to let you use their bathroom
- ☐ Attaching things to your belt
- ☐ Pointing out counterintuitive safety facts ("You're actually better off in the epicenter of the blast zone!")

YOU ARE GOOD AT BOWLING ALLEY EMPLOYEE THINGS

- ☐ Appreciating retro signage

- ☐ Enforcing the no-practice-frame policy

- ☐ Deciding when old house balls no longer meet the basic definition of a sphere

- ☐ Shaking your head ruefully at kids who don't know how to keep score by hand

- ☐ Knowing when street shoes being traded in aren't enough collateral

- ☐ Not falling for it when people call and ask if you have 14-pound balls

- ☐ Assuring uneasy customers that a quick spritz of antibaterial spray in the vague direction of a rental shoe is an effective sterilization method

- ☐ Pointing out that just because you can bowl while drinking beer and eating nachos doesn't mean it's not a sport

- ☐ Quoting from *The Big Lebowski* and *Kingpin*

- ☐ Being hardened to the broken dreams of double dates when you tell them it's league night

- ☐ Reminiscing about the golden age of the pinboy

- ☐ Not giggling when people ask for ball polish

- ☐ Waiting for your buddies
- ☐ Checking local listings for details, and acting on them
- ☐ Wielding squeegees
- ☐ Paying what you wish
- ☐ Dramatically pressing cans of cold drinks against your forehead
- ☐ Finding scraps of paper to wrap chewed gum in
- ☐ Thinking of original places to stick name tags and museum admissions stickers
- ☐ Sifting and winnowing
- ☐ Inspecting restaurant flatware for mystery globs
- ☐ Extracting Jell-O shots
- ☐ Coaxing reluctant ice cubes from paper cups
- ☐ Making elaborate crayon drawings on paper tablecloths
- ☐ Taking advantage of found hopscotch courts
- ☐ Having tentative dinner plans
- ☐ Being an aficionado
- ☐ Bobbing for apples
- ☐ Keeping your seatbelt low and tight across your lap
- ☐ Counting crows
- ☐ Flying under the radar (literally)
- ☐ Flying under the radar (figuratively)
- ☐ Maintaining vacuums
- ☐ Interpreting washing and drying instruction symbols

- ☐ Forgetting everything you've ever learned
- ☐ Working out the kinks
- ☐ Making good time
- ☐ Mowing precisely along your property line
- ☐ Knowing precisely where your property line is
- ☐ Sensing when the dental floss spool is nearing its end
- ☐ Notifying maintenance
- ☐ Changing discreetly under a towel
- ☐ Changing discreetly in public restrooms
- ☐ Tweaking your hit tribute song to memorialize someone else
- ☐ Understanding why the movie version was necessary
- ☐ Snagging a table while somebody else orders
- ☐ Redirecting lust in productive directions
- ☐ Knowing which side to err on
- ☐ Liking products so much that you buy the company
- ☐ Sticking up for the little guy
- ☐ Sticking it to the little guy
- ☐ Raising Cain
- ☐ Raising the roof
- ☐ Raising the bar
- ☐ Raising kids

- [ ] Putting the moves on
- [ ] Seeing the resemblance
- [ ] Having a way with words
- [ ] Letting words have their way with you
- [ ] Using mnemonic devices
- [ ] Getting picked up by all the major media outlets
- [ ] Using unconventional salad ingredients
- [ ] Denouncing Ticketmaster before going ahead and paying their fees anyway
- [ ] Imagining yourself living in houses you pass
- [ ] Standing for something
- [ ] Falling for nothing
- [ ] Checking your reflection out in car windows
- [ ] Leaving things unsaid
- [ ] Knowing when a school shirt represents the wearer's actual alma mater
- [ ] Coming up with fresh "You can't spell 'grime' without 'me'" type sayings
- [ ] Scaring all the fish away
- [ ] Falling from grace
- [ ] Aggressively enforcing drink toast rituals
- [ ] Letting straps fall seductively off your shoulder
- [ ] Blowing your top
- [ ] Counting slowly to ten instead of blowing your top

☐ Having appropriate expressions while watching sex scenes

- ☐ Yelling at the TV
- ☐ Racing against the clock
- ☐ Shoveling without injuring your back
- ☐ Depending on the kindness of strangers
- ☐ Being a kind stranger on whom others depend
- ☐ Adding up your score
- ☐ Being a stickler about differentiating between barbed wire, razor wire, and concertina wire
- ☐ Identifying herbs
- ☐ Maneuvering strollers
- ☐ Showing off
- ☐ Showing up
- ☐ Showing your true colors
- ☐ Showing how it's done
- ☐ Knowing when the generic is sufficient
- ☐ Knowing the right Bible verses to share at sporting events
- ☐ Taking it all in
- ☐ Fighting the good fight
- ☐ Fighting the questionable fight
- ☐ Straightening out messes
- ☐ Giving hairstylists clear instructions
- ☐ Spitting only in garbage cans
- ☐ Knowing of what you speak
- ☐ Not flinching

- [ ] Yelling original prompts at improv shows
- [ ] Pacing yourself at buffets
- [ ] Knowing when "Open" signs have merely been left on and do not reflect actual openness
- [ ] Conveying your cultural standing through tote bags
- [ ] Altering prayers so they read as gender neutral
- [ ] Somehow knowing precisely what you, and others, will and won't regret on a deathbed
- [ ] Deciding which doughnut you want with briskness and confidence
- [ ] Keeping hermit crabs alive for a really long time
- [ ] Coming up with creative ways to swear in front of little kids
- [ ] Repressing painful memories
- [ ] Showing extraordinary brand loyalty
- [ ] Embracing theme nights at bars and clubs
- [ ] Having an unguessable sexual orientation
- [ ] Notifying attendants
- [ ] Saving receipts
- [ ] Collecting signatures
- [ ] Not being fully appreciated in your hometown
- [ ] Using the recipes on the back of the package
- [ ] Not swatting too wildly when there's a buzzing in your ear
- [ ] Apologizing for not getting back to people sooner

☐ Getting animals to look cute on camera

- [ ] Rating your transactions
- [ ] Having ideas for things we should make instead of war
- [ ] Asking people where they learned to dance like that
- [ ] Making a mockery of the proceedings
- [ ] Getting fruit cup ratios right
- [ ] Sleeping in papasan chairs
- [ ] Letting it be known when you contribute to the tip jar
- [ ] Teaching people how to burp at will
- [ ] Keeping your place on X-Y graphs
- [ ] Finding headphones that don't pop out while exercising
- [ ] Fixing zippers
- [ ] Hosting pay-per-view events at your place
- [ ] Swaying during concerts
- [ ] Having ringtones that give people pause
- [ ] Being on top of fad diets
- [ ] Reading deep truths into the way people part their hair
- [ ] Waiting until they iron out the bugs
- [ ] Winning at the claw crane
- [ ] Not being confined to one genre
- [ ] Convincing people to have extramarital affairs with you
- [ ] Going on to do interesting things
- [ ] Keeping track of all the neighborhood pets

- ☐ Winning at correspondence chess
- ☐ Winning at correspondence
- ☐ Goofing around on playgrounds after hours
- ☐ Differentiating between lummoxes and galoots
- ☐ Checking sports scores discreetly
- ☐ Setting agendas
- ☐ Taking cautionary tales to heart
- ☐ Sparking firestorms of debate
- ☐ Starting limbos
- ☐ Maintaining a half-tucked-in look
- ☐ Taking care of children while still being one yourself
- ☐ Sensing when something is different but not being able to put your finger on precisely what's different about it
- ☐ Estimating how many stitches different cuts will require
- ☐ Reusing Ziploc bags
- ☐ Showing no fear
- ☐ Showing appropriate amounts of fear
- ☐ Adjusting for inflation
- ☐ Putting things on kebabs that were previously thought to be unkebabable
- ☐ Scoring the company's box seats
- ☐ Figuring in tax and shipping
- ☐ Multitasking
- ☐ Monotasking

☐ Asking friends if they'd be up for surrogate motherhood

- [ ] Contemplating the oneness of all things
- [ ] Contemplating the irreconcilable manyness of all things
- [ ] Bear-hugging
- [ ] Waiting for the passenger door to be fully unlocked before yanking on the handle
- [ ] Hitting the ground running
- [ ] Becoming what you despise
- [ ] Going to their website for additional information
- [ ] Intentionally mispronouncing things, like popular bands or shows, so it doesn't seem like you know about them
- [ ] Eating things like popcorn (meaning, eating things in a manner similar to how one normally eats popcorn)
- [ ] Overtreating scraped knees
- [ ] Finding things to lock bikes to
- [ ] Applying makeup while riding the subway
- [ ] Applying makeup while driving
- [ ] Shaking people down
- [ ] Guessing what's in presents by shaking them
- [ ] Scanning crowds for people of interest
- [ ] Breaking up fights
- [ ] Engaging in self-promotion
- [ ] Engaging in self-demotion

- [ ] Feeling wistful about old soda logos
- [ ] Communicating your appreciation by whistling
- [ ] Opening doors while carrying things
- [ ] Conveying nuance in car horn honks
- [ ] Dressing down blazers
- [ ] Remembering old candies
- [ ] Remembering old candy prices
- [ ] Pointing out where they make their money
- [ ] Ignoring the signs (traffic)
- [ ] Ignoring the signs (romantic)
- [ ] Ignoring the signs (cosmic)
- [ ] Adding extra belt holes that look natural
- [ ] Paraphrasing
- [ ] Achieving greatness
- [ ] Enjoying the silence
- [ ] Winning most-improved awards
- [ ] Knowing when you've had enough
- [ ] Not acting too eager in front of the mailman
- [ ] Subtly signaling people when they have food in their teeth
- [ ] Picking up on subtle signals that you have food in your teeth

- ☐ Admitting that maybe you were too harsh
- ☐ Cleaning up your act
- ☐ Untangling dogs from leashes
- ☐ Being a parking coach
- ☐ Taking hints
- ☐ Forming brat packs
- ☐ Never letting them see the real you
- ☐ Packing the courts
- ☐ Packing wallops
- ☐ Politely requesting drumrolls
- ☐ Feeling sorry for yourself
- ☐ Going through other people's yearbooks and pointing out who's hot
- ☐ Strutting your stuff
- ☐ Skirting issues
- ☐ Laying blame
- ☐ Archiving footage
- ☐ Coming clean
- ☐ Separating chopsticks cleanly
- ☐ Keeping streaks alive
- ☐ Working the phrase "This used to be all cornfield" into tours of the old neighborhood

☐ Peeking at people's electronic devices without being too obvious about it

- ☐ Pumping up the jam
- ☐ Sticking stickers
- ☐ Clipping toenails straight across
- ☐ Speaking truth to power
- ☐ Telling power what it wants to hear
- ☐ Busting rhymes
- ☐ Taking it outside
- ☐ Mishearing lyrics so that your version's better than the real one
- ☐ Turning regular sentences into poetry with unconventional line breaks
- ☐ Catching drifts
- ☐ Knowing things without Internet assistance
- ☐ Trying on cheap sunglasses like you're in a movie montage
- ☐ Accusing people of being drunk when they are actually suffering from a neurological disorder
- ☐ Asking if it's to scale
- ☐ Usefully drawing on what little Spanish you remember from high school
- ☐ Keeping the line moving
- ☐ Loving the one you're with
- ☐ Blaming your racket
- ☐ Just walking away
- ☐ Emancipating yourself from mental slavery

- ☐ Consuming conspicuously
- ☐ Consuming on the down-low
- ☐ Always having a secret ingredient
- ☐ Knowing the exceptions to spelling and grammar rules
- ☐ Being off in your own little world
- ☐ Knowing who your real friends are
- ☐ Throwing old helium balloons away before they get too depressing
- ☐ Spotting two-way mirrors
- ☐ Getting plucked from obscurity
- ☐ Whispering at the correct angle in whisper chambers
- ☐ Extending elaborate, public marriage proposals
- ☐ Declining elaborate, public marriage proposals
- ☐ Obeying low speed limits
- ☐ Risking everything for the truth
- ☐ Talking about what everybody's talking about
- ☐ Figuring out who's in charge here
- ☐ Noting quality bone structure
- ☐ Never letting them see you sweat
- ☐ Sweating theatrically
- ☐ Always sitting with your back to the wall in restaurants
- ☐ Announcing grandly that you always sit with your back to the wall in restaurants

- ☐ Being careful not to insult people by denouncing their artificial sweetener of choice
- ☐ Having a precise sense of when things are shoulder-width apart
- ☐ Letting kids be kids
- ☐ Being dubious of "Wet Paint" signs
- ☐ Rhapsodizing about the glory of summer dresses
- ☐ Figuring out what song is playing just from hearing the tinny noise from someone else's headphones
- ☐ Not backing down when you've gotten yourself into sexual escapades way beyond your comfort zone
- ☐ Forcing people to answer absurd hypothetical questions
- ☐ Always having spare money in your sock
- ☐ Not getting grossed out when people pay you with sock money
- ☐ Letting the story be told
- ☐ Knowing when you can and can't call people "dear"
- ☐ Understanding the appeal
- ☐ Treating people as ends rather than means
- ☐ Refusing to compromise your artistic vision
- ☐ Refusing to compromise your nonartistic vision
- ☐ Taking leaflets to be polite
- ☐ Noting when things aren't everything, they're the only thing
- ☐ Remaining alert

☐ Cutting the grass before it gets too long

- [ ] Using "Euro" as a prefix
- [ ] Sensing when places are cash only
- [ ] Helping people help themselves
- [ ] Knowing when to draw the line
- [ ] Knowing where to draw the line
- [ ] Knowing how to draw the line
- [ ] Catching keys thrown from windows
- [ ] Not getting clunked by keys thrown from windows
- [ ] Working "Webster's defines" into speeches
- [ ] Establishing beachheads
- [ ] Teaching your parents well
- [ ] Not being afraid to collect rewards for finding lost pets
- [ ] Waxing philosophic about visible panty lines
- [ ] Getting all dolled up
- [ ] Asking "Is that so wrong?" before or after doing things that are clearly wrong
- [ ] Putting extra leaves in the table
- [ ] Writing "(sp?)" rather than looking up how a word is spelled
- [ ] Starting semesters in style
- [ ] Playing it cool
- [ ] Playing it uncool
- [ ] Using the phrase "This is why we can never have nice things"

- [ ] Quitting solitaire when you're ahead
- [ ] Playing the blame game to win
- [ ] Playing the blame game as a lighthearted scrimmage
- [ ] Telling strangers when a clothing tag is showing
- [ ] Liking a one-hit-wonder band's other songs
- [ ] Searching for signals
- [ ] Believing in yourself, despite an overwhelming lack of evidence
- [ ] Keeping in touch with your law school chums
- [ ] Keeping in touch with your old army buddies
- [ ] Trilling r's
- [ ] Trilling letters other than r
- [ ] Sensing which side of the street an address will be on
- [ ] Hacking into mainframes
- [ ] Letting paint peel just so
- [ ] Converting people to things other than religions
- [ ] Knowing what all the symbolic bracelets mean
- [ ] Finding places other than your shirt to wipe your nose
- [ ] Finding places other than your pants to wipe your hands
- [ ] Knowing whether these times are trying
- [ ] Sketching billion-dollar ideas on cocktail napkins
- [ ] Using cocktail napkins as a buffer between cocktails and wood surfaces
- [ ] Using cocktails napkins as regular napkins

YOU ARE GOOD AT
GOOD-FOR-NOTHING THINGS

- ☐ Combining different cereals into one bowl to minimize awareness of your cereal consumption

- ☐ Conveniently forgetting your wallet

- ☐ Staying late enough where it would be unsafe to not let you stay over

- ☐ Explaining why jobs didn't work out

- ☐ Pretending to go on job interviews

- ☐ Leveraging roguish charm

- ☐ Vowing to change your ways

- ☐ Shielding your head with your arms while people who believed you were going to change your ways throw things at you

- ☐ Not doing dishes

- ☐ Talking utilities into not cutting off service

- ☐ Forcing a host to quietly get ready for work as you sleep on the couch

- ☐ Leaving a college course catalog around to show you're thinking about it

- ☐ Making one spectacular meal that gets everybody off your back for a while

- ☐ Getting all worked up
- ☐ Advising people not to get all worked up in such a way that gets them even more worked up
- ☐ Not racking up massive communications device bills when traveling out of the country
- ☐ Blaming the government
- ☐ Blaming yourself
- ☐ Blaming your parents
- ☐ Settling out of court
- ☐ Spotting holes in plots of time-travel movies
- ☐ Praying in public
- ☐ Allowing for error
- ☐ Knowing if there's an app for that
- ☐ Not counting small things, like cigarette butts and gum wrappers, as litter
- ☐ Taking care to count small things, like cigarette butts and toothpick wrappers, as litter
- ☐ Maintaining a sense of childlike wonder
- ☐ Ditching your sense of childlike wonder and picking up a sense of steely-eyed cynicism
- ☐ Repurposing plastic cat litter containers
- ☐ Pointing out when people are damaging their cars with bad driving habits
- ☐ Customizing templates
- ☐ Staying awake for midnight movies

☐ Making people wonder whether your outdoor showers are about personal hygiene or erotic exhibitionism

- ☐ Not believing the hype
- ☐ Succumbing joyfully to the hype
- ☐ Beckoning
- ☐ Allowing yourself to be beckoned
- ☐ Saying, "Yes, Your Highness"
- ☐ Tossing your tie over your shoulder while eating
- ☐ Confining use of the word "addiction" to describe true chemical dependencies
- ☐ Being able to tell the difference between jars of apple juice and urine
- ☐ Always having a fresh euphemism for "dead"
- ☐ Coming up with neat things to use as bookmarks
- ☐ Sending in religious conversion narratives for the reunion booklet
- ☐ Finding something other than cigarettes to keep in that great old cigarette case
- ☐ Making a real effort to look for faces you see on "Missing" posters
- ☐ Thinking of yourself as someone who adheres to an ancient warrior code
- ☐ Adding "of the mind" to things (e.g., "You must clean out the lint trap of the mind")
- ☐ Buying lottery tickets only when the jackpot is over a specific amount
- ☐ Knowing when treating a stain will only make it worse
- ☐ Railing against cineplexes

- ☐ Feeling okay about the fact that all of this will be gone some day
- ☐ Always having a go-bag ready
- ☐ Booing subpar performances
- ☐ Feeling nostalgia for the old ways of fighting wars
- ☐ Getting accepted at unfamiliar biker bars
- ☐ Coming up with puns for new haircut-place names ("Hair Ye! Hair Ye! We Are Scissored Here Today")
- ☐ Drawing a blank
- ☐ Drawing blanks with startling vividness and accuracy
- ☐ Ejecting before disconnecting
- ☐ Putting together great workout mixes
- ☐ Putting together great makeout mixes
- ☐ Overcoming your fears
- ☐ Letting your fears overcome you
- ☐ Flirting with disaster
- ☐ Making out with disaster
- ☐ Knowing when bartenders are flirting with you for real vs. for-tip-real
- ☐ Acting on betting tips
- ☐ Stocking the cabin with old toys and boring books
- ☐ Not falling prey to guerrilla marketing schemes
- ☐ Getting mad at inanimate objects
- ☐ Modifying the classic Philly cheesesteak
- ☐ Keeping your stories straight

☐ Encouraging friends to put up online dating profiles

- [ ] Haggling at lemonade stands
- [ ] Commenting on the strength of people's glasses prescriptions
- [ ] Looking alive out there
- [ ] Always having an extra helmet for guest riders
- [ ] Feeding the meter
- [ ] Flashing a little skin
- [ ] Declaring moratoriums
- [ ] Letting people know when their sock choice isn't working
- [ ] Shutting up before somebody shuts you up
- [ ] Dividing your time
- [ ] Setting up shop
- [ ] Encouraging sustainable growth
- [ ] Stopping before you're full
- [ ] Sharing headphones
- [ ] Catching all the NFL action
- [ ] Holding on to the right business cards
- [ ] Cutting up apples with a pocketknife
- [ ] Telling better from worse when it gets really close in eye tests
- [ ] Keeping cargo in your cargo shorts
- [ ] Knowing exactly what time it is before opening your eyes and looking at the alarm clock

- [ ] Letting everyone know how tired you are
- [ ] Letting everyone know how awake you are
- [ ] Starting drum circles
- [ ] Joining drum circles
- [ ] Mocking drum circles
- [ ] Peeling magazine subscription labels off
- [ ] Knowing what to shred and what to crumple
- [ ] Denouncing overly emotional charity ads
- [ ] Getting exempted from "please remove your shoes" rules
- [ ] Having lucky numbers
- [ ] Having really specific cravings
- [ ] Sating really specific cravings
- [ ] Starting out strict
- [ ] Knowing which product tags are cool to leave on
- [ ] Giving desperate times whatever it is that they demand
- [ ] Not giving them the satisfaction
- [ ] Carrying things in the crook of your arm
- [ ] Retooling old Henny Youngman jokes
- [ ] Knowing what people could and couldn't pay you to do
- [ ] Knowing which compartment of your backpack everything is in

- ☐ Getting really mad when you think people are taking pictures of you
- ☐ Using stickers to announce the accomplishment of deeds like voting and giving blood
- ☐ Stockpiling
- ☐ Knowing whether to apply a hot pad or a cold compress
- ☐ Asking for Wi-Fi passwords
- ☐ Trading up
- ☐ Trading down
- ☐ Pulling rank
- ☐ Living on the edge
- ☐ Living in the middle
- ☐ Getting picked to participate in magic shows and street dance performances
- ☐ Always having a pretty good idea for whom the bell is tolling
- ☐ Bluffing
- ☐ Resembling others
- ☐ Repurposing zingers from old presidential debates
- ☐ Asking people to sock it to you
- ☐ Socking it to people on request
- ☐ Calling bluffs
- ☐ Letting bluffs be
- ☐ Heading out by the bluffs and contemplating time

☐ Driving no-handed

- [ ] Getting friends to stay up past their bedtimes
- [ ] Staying late and helping clean up
- [ ] Coming up with things for subjects to say other than "cheese" when taking group portraits
- [ ] Talking kids into liking their freckles
- [ ] Talking kids into liking their curly hair
- [ ] Popping that shoulder back into place
- [ ] Refilling the water bottle
- [ ] Never passing up an opportunity to use an in-store blood pressure machine
- [ ] Urinating while other people are in the room
- [ ] Getting your foot to fall asleep at will
- [ ] Doing your own stunts
- [ ] Feeling sorry for bugs
- [ ] Whistleblowing (referee/gym)
- [ ] Whistleblowing (unveiling corruption)
- [ ] Whistleblowing (party favor)
- [ ] Sticking to the training regimen
- [ ] Letting the regimen go when necessary
- [ ] Seductively pushing sunglasses up the bridge of your nose
- [ ] Seductively biting your bottom lip
- [ ] Switching storm windows in and out in a timely fashion
- [ ] Breaking in baseball gloves
- [ ] Getting in lines even when you don't know what the line is for

- ☐ Taking strolls
- ☐ Reparking when an orginal park job is sloppy
- ☐ Passing along people's best when asked
- ☐ Not confusing Icees, Slurpees, and Slush Puppies
- ☐ Not being intimidated by the selection at the fancy cheese shop
- ☐ Menacingly suggesting that people wait until they get a load of you
- ☐ Leveraging customer service hotlines for free samples
- ☐ Breaking it to them gently
- ☐ Knowing infinite variations on the push-up
- ☐ Walking with your hand in a date's back pocket
- ☐ Blinking and missing it
- ☐ Waiting until the last second to swoop into a crowded exit lane
- ☐ Rescheduling
- ☐ Knowing what entrance to use at the stadium
- ☐ Adhering to all the tenets of high-end denim care
- ☐ Outsmarting ankle monitors
- ☐ Knowing which types of animals like or don't like you
- ☐ Watching your weight
- ☐ Watching others' weights
- ☐ Rolling up your pants just so
- ☐ Using the phrase "just so" just so

☐ Figuring when it's *probably* okay to accept painkillers from people you don't know very well

- [ ] Asking couples how they met
- [ ] Telling people you find attractive to "Take it off!"
- [ ] Taking it off upon request
- [ ] Pointing out when coincidences aren't all that amazing, mathematically
- [ ] Knowing the precise force and duration of a "proper" spanking
- [ ] Walking with a jacket flung over your shoulder
- [ ] Applying fishing wisdom to regular life
- [ ] Knowing the profit margins on *everything*
- [ ] Seducing with sonnets
- [ ] Repelling with sonnets
- [ ] Feeling outrage when radio stations censor profanity or drug references in songs
- [ ] Actually saying, "Aw, shucks"
- [ ] Seething
- [ ] Pointing out when great-seeming things are actually a curse
- [ ] Unhooking bras
- [ ] Sculpting demonic-looking facial hair
- [ ] Pointing out landmarks
- [ ] Giving hickeys
- [ ] Creatively covering up hickeys
- [ ] Wearing hickeys with pride

- [ ] Getting it over with
- [ ] Knowing the *-icide* to describe every type of murder
- [ ] Making it up as you go along
- [ ] Accepting that which you cannot change
- [ ] Wresting away the remote
- [ ] Snooping
- [ ] Explaining how sound travels
- [ ] Tightening the screws (assembly/repair)
- [ ] Tightening the screws (interrogation)
- [ ] Yelling for public speakers to talk louder
- [ ] Having a loose idea of what constitutes holy ground
- [ ] Being, like, whatever
- [ ] Pointing out that "Chinese" isn't actually a language
- [ ] Doing noncelebrity impressions
- [ ] Assuring discretion
- [ ] Doing lots of online product research before making a $10 investment
- [ ] Removing staples without an official remover
- [ ] Using "Hey, buddy" to get somebody's attention
- [ ] Knowing what you want and going after it
- [ ] Knowing what you want and reveling in the state of wanting
- [ ] Subverting the dominant paradigm
- [ ] Upholding the dominant paradigm

YOU ARE GOOD AT WORKING FROM HOME THINGS

- ☐ Typing one-handed
- ☐ Taking breaks
- ☐ Prioritizing household chores over making a living
- ☐ Convincing people that you actually have a job
- ☐ Explaining to your kids why you can't play with them even though you're home
- ☐ Explaining to your spouse why you won't be able to let the cable guy in even though you'll be around
- ☐ Putting on shoes so you don't accidentally go back to bed
- ☐ Knowing exactly when the cat will nudge you for dinner
- ☐ Knowing exactly when the dog will beg for a walk
- ☐ Treating the trip to the post office as a social occasion
- ☐ Determining which errands require a shirt that hasn't been slept in
- ☐ Knowing the neighbor's schedule
- ☐ Pushing the boundaries of the phrase "business casual"
- ☐ Knowing what day of the week it is, sometimes

- ☐ Covering the spread
- ☐ Letting the spread cover you
- ☐ Reversing statements so they sound profound
- ☐ Easing on down the road
- ☐ Letting people know when they don't know you
- ☐ Expressing the inexpressible
- ☐ Pouting
- ☐ Vouching
- ☐ Mixing business with pleasure
- ☐ Finding your way back
- ☐ Being a study buddy
- ☐ Confining your portion to the recommended serving size
- ☐ Strapping yourself in
- ☐ Drying the insides of your ears
- ☐ Chalking pool cues
- ☐ Navigating wine lists
- ☐ Mincing words
- ☐ Giving gifts that increase in sentimental value
- ☐ Dealing with hangnails
- ☐ Having a system
- ☐ Creating distractions
- ☐ Slinking away

☐ Knowing whether flowing all-white outfits indicate cult membership or a fashion preference

- ☐ Instigating celebratory Gatorade dumps
- ☐ Being enthusiastic about jury duty
- ☐ Aerating soil
- ☐ Levitating
- ☐ Knowing when shifting holidays fall
- ☐ Panning (movies/restaurants)
- ☐ Panning (for gold)
- ☐ Wearing hoods in a way that isn't menacing
- ☐ Making things a beacon unto others
- ☐ Securing takeout coffee lids
- ☐ Mellowing with age
- ☐ Calcifying into a ball of rage with age
- ☐ Pre-partying
- ☐ Expanding the boundaries of sandal season
- ☐ Managing tongue twisters
- ☐ Leaving people in the lurch
- ☐ Rescuing people from the lurch
- ☐ Waiting for the rain to let up
- ☐ Making people feel really bad about being unfamiliar with your favorite sketch comedy show
- ☐ Getting all your protein in shake form

- ☐ Hazing
- ☐ Extracting drawstrings
- ☐ Making seating charts
- ☐ Staying just the way you are
- ☐ Running things up flagpoles
- ☐ Changing behind screens so your silhouette is visible
- ☐ Asking the group to wait up
- ☐ Waiting up
- ☐ Getting suspended instead of expelled for your shenanigans
- ☐ Just putting it out there
- ☐ Making things really awkward around here
- ☐ Making sure people use drink coasters
- ☐ Making sandwiches for the road
- ☐ Appreciating the irony
- ☐ Sucking it up
- ☐ Managing lint
- ☐ Sweeping things under the rug (literally)
- ☐ Sweeping things under the rug (figuratively)
- ☐ Knowing what's gauche
- ☐ Loafing
- ☐ Telling people they worry too much
- ☐ Worrying too much

- ☐ Having classy outfits in your school colors
- ☐ Getting just the right arc in baseball cap rims
- ☐ Saving dates
- ☐ Having a bead on the season's hot Halloween costume
- ☐ Going all the way
- ☐ Finding secret, possibly nonexistent, drug references
- ☐ Remembering who you've already told which stories to
- ☐ Taking mental notes
- ☐ Deciphering mental shorthand
- ☐ Finding chill sports bars
- ☐ Taking showers right before bed
- ☐ Being the envy of all your friends
- ☐ Envying all your friends
- ☐ Having rad bike accessories
- ☐ Getting an early start
- ☐ Beating the traffic
- ☐ Letting the traffic beat you
- ☐ Reminding people that there's no such thing as a free lunch
- ☐ Constantly correcting your posture
- ☐ Making out in the back row

- [ ] Being hip to the latest methods of baby lugging
- [ ] Not letting funeral directors up-sell you
- [ ] Checking for swollen lymph nodes
- [ ] Accentuating the positive
- [ ] Promptly adjusting watches for new time zones when traveling
- [ ] Knowing which supernatural figure is in the details
- [ ] Claiming you saw it first
- [ ] Using the word "primo" to good effect
- [ ] Getting magicians to reveal their secrets
- [ ] Reading body language
- [ ] Rigging pulley systems
- [ ] Fashioning crude versions of advanced technologies using only the materials at hand
- [ ] Broadening your horizons
- [ ] Playing patty-cake
- [ ] Doing chair-based exercises
- [ ] Keeping the Beatles vs. Stones debate alive
- [ ] Sensing when it is or isn't okay to ask for a second helping
- [ ] Deftly folding strollers
- [ ] Tactfully letting people know when they have bad breath

☐ Carrying as much as possible before getting a grocery cart

- ☐ Nursing drinks
- ☐ Knowing when to cut your elevator-waiting losses and take the stairs
- ☐ Patching things up (clothing)
- ☐ Patching things up (relationships)
- ☐ Patching things up (with patch cords)
- ☐ Stowing away
- ☐ Amassing airline miles
- ☐ Letting people know when you flew using miles
- ☐ Daubing
- ☐ Being there but not there
- ☐ Embracing food fads
- ☐ Working other people's coffeemakers without asking for instructions
- ☐ Pronouncing the names of foreign designers correctly
- ☐ Distributing weight evenly
- ☐ Warbling
- ☐ Knowing where all the hot spots are (nightlife)
- ☐ Knowing where all the hot spots are (Wi-Fi)
- ☐ Knowing where all the hot spots are (temperature)
- ☐ Convincing people that they're aging like a fine wine
- ☐ Figuring out the name of the song that was in that preview

- [ ] Wondering where you went wrong
- [ ] Having a pretty solid idea of where you went wrong
- [ ] Hard-boiling eggs just so
- [ ] Issuing "nerd alerts"
- [ ] Responding to "nerd alerts"
- [ ] Replacing worn socks
- [ ] Dodging comeuppance
- [ ] Cheating on eye tests
- [ ] Criticizing what you can't understand
- [ ] Slouching toward things
- [ ] Being honest about how you came out at the track
- [ ] Force-quitting computer programs
- [ ] Signing yearbooks and guestbooks with heartfelt and original quips
- [ ] Stretching out countdowns
- [ ] Making innocent transactions look and feel illicit
- [ ] Presenting tastes of stew on wooden spoons
- [ ] Jumper-cabling
- [ ] Noting when "There can be only one"
- [ ] Coming up with ingenious iterations on "Roses are red . . ."
- [ ] Portraying yourself as a populist outsider
- [ ] Asking people, "What, you got something better to do?"
- [ ] Asking people, "What, you got someplace better to be?"

- [ ] Keeping busy
- [ ] Marking territory
- [ ] Announcing when it's time to bring out the big guns
- [ ] Wearing suits when no one else does
- [ ] Tweaking the school uniform to make it your own
- [ ] Checking your blind spot
- [ ] Having unexpectedly impressive muscle definition
- [ ] Seducing via hands-on golf swing instruction
- [ ] Breaking boards with your hand
- [ ] Breaking cinder blocks with your forehead
- [ ] Proposing pizza topping compromises acceptable to all
- [ ] Deciding when picture frames are straight
- [ ] Insinuating yourself
- [ ] Misting things
- [ ] Not being afraid to ask people about their teardrop tattoos
- [ ] Complaining about invasive communications technologies that most folks got used to ten years ago
- [ ] Surveying the scene
- [ ] Playing against type
- [ ] Expecting the unexpected
- [ ] Expecting the expected
- [ ] Designating drivers

- [ ] Tasting victory
- [ ] Not putting a label on whatever this is
- [ ] Carrying on "'Fraid not!" "'Fraid so!" arguments for a long time
- [ ] Defending fruitcake
- [ ] Defending fruitcakes
- [ ] Coming to an understanding
- [ ] Radiating joy
- [ ] Just getting it done
- [ ] Having gigantic binder clips
- [ ] Saying "If I do say so myself" after saying things
- [ ] Ragging on things that everyone likes
- [ ] Declaring open seasons
- [ ] Bemoaning the demise of true manhood
- [ ] Celebrating the demise of true manhood
- [ ] Arraying your degrees and awards impressively on a wall behind your desk
- [ ] Reading along silently while an authority figure reads aloud
- [ ] Getting eyeglasses that convey your profession
- [ ] Defining snark
- [ ] Not getting frequently confused words confused (e.g., "etymology" and "entymology")
- [ ] Referring to name-changing celebrities by their most recent name

☐ Sharing food without making everyone else around un-
comfortable

- ☐ Making courtesy calls
- ☐ Putting together demolition crews
- ☐ Believing in the healing power of art
- ☐ Getting permanent marker off dry-erase boards
- ☐ Having the sea do all your dirty work
- ☐ Noting when things are unexpectedly moving
- ☐ Feeling like you've been here before
- ☐ Being philosophical about traffic
- ☐ Accepting your own mortality
- ☐ Accepting others' mortality
- ☐ Just being glad to be on the team
- ☐ Raising a stink
- ☐ Using "crazy" as a modifier (e.g., "That drum solo is crazy inspiring"; "Your toddler is crazy cute"; "My quads are crazy sore")
- ☐ Drizzling sauces
- ☐ Knowing when to break out the leopard print
- ☐ Assuming people talking into their headsets are talking to you
- ☐ Thinking of master plans
- ☐ Putting master plans into action
- ☐ Using wrist straps

- ☐ Chiding kids for being more excited about the box than the gift inside
- ☐ Not stepping on cracks
- ☐ Stepping on cracks
- ☐ Commandeering booths in diners
- ☐ Holding forth
- ☐ Holding back
- ☐ Knowing when it's time for critical reassessments of maligned works
- ☐ Asking people if they're high
- ☐ Dismissing things as mere popularity contests
- ☐ Being clever, but not frightfully so
- ☐ Ponying up dough
- ☐ Wearing things bandolier-style
- ☐ Not being so obvious about it
- ☐ Careening
- ☐ Acknowledging those small but precious bonding moments between strangers
- ☐ Texting precise descriptions of your location so people can find you in crowds
- ☐ Illuminating the darker corners of the human soul
- ☐ Darkening the brighter corners of the human soul
- ☐ Knowing what the initials in car models stand for
- ☐ Browning things evenly on all sides

☐ Plugging your ears the old-fashioned way

- [ ] Playing along
- [ ] Pretending to understand what's going on
- [ ] Being convinced that the urban legend you're passing on is true because it happened to a friend of your aunt
- [ ] Being a news program's go-to commentator for some weirdly specific thing
- [ ] Pointing out that many classic children's stories contain extreme violence
- [ ] Making love in the grass
- [ ] Silencing people with just a look
- [ ] Considering yourself a falafel connoisseur
- [ ] Switching sides
- [ ] Taking ganders
- [ ] Calling shotgun
- [ ] Declaring thumb wars
- [ ] Harumphing
- [ ] Seeing all without looking
- [ ] Doing all without moving
- [ ] Owning all without having
- [ ] Cursing all without swearing
- [ ] Threatening to sue over uneven sidewalks
- [ ] Threatening to countersue
- [ ] Dressing appropriately for black lighting

- [ ] Leading a secret double life
- [ ] Finding spaces with time left on the meter
- [ ] Hanging tough
- [ ] Winning gross-out contests
- [ ] Taking "No Loitering" signs seriously
- [ ] Turning -ophobes into -ophiles
- [ ] Getting really common phrases trademarked
- [ ] Luring people into your lair
- [ ] Tricking out your lair
- [ ] Stacking decks
- [ ] Only using superlatives when you really mean them
- [ ] Being familiar with the mass transit systems of many cities
- [ ] Speaking in triple and quadruple negatives
- [ ] Taking double negatives seriously
- [ ] Knowing what comes after quintuple
- [ ] Bringing maritime terminology to land
- [ ] Having a really impressive stack of magazines on the coffee table
- [ ] Maintaining a state of attractive dishevelment
- [ ] Vilifying industries by adding the descriptor "big" (e.g., "I ate more dried fruit before everything was taken over by Big Fig")
- [ ] Conveying the precise nature of an unpleasant smell via facial expression

- [ ] Working "You seem like a reasonable man" into arguments
- [ ] Finding pass-along newspapers
- [ ] Not letting child stardom ruin you
- [ ] Sensing when chairs are stackable
- [ ] Coming up with good subject lines for emails
- [ ] Hiding house keys
- [ ] Going ridiculously far to avoid dangling participles
- [ ] Selecting pumpkins
- [ ] Decorating paper lunch bags
- [ ] Helping your kids just enough so their school projects are respectable and they learn something
- [ ] Getting excited when your initials turn up unexpectedly
- [ ] Being eligible for medical trials
- [ ] Holding it until the next rest stop
- [ ] Giving it all away
- [ ] Opting for dishonor before death
- [ ] Letting your open coat blow in the wind
- [ ] Instantly knowing whether people are talking about space aliens or other-country aliens
- [ ] Telling people seeing triple to go for the one in the middle
- [ ] Bringing bikes on public transportation
- [ ] Refilling water bottles
- [ ] Applying early

- ☐ Taking care to hate the game and not the player
- ☐ Being up on the latest superfoods
- ☐ Finding and removing printer misfeeds
- ☐ Using scare tactics
- ☐ Using soothe tactics
- ☐ Using old restaurant lingo
- ☐ Pshawing
- ☐ Keeping Yiddish alive
- ☐ Snagging the honorable discharge
- ☐ Specifying when you're not asking, you're telling
- ☐ Destroying things in order to save them
- ☐ Emulsifying
- ☐ Using hotel lobbies at hotels where you aren't staying
- ☐ Rehearsing awards acceptance speeches
- ☐ Throwing your weight around
- ☐ Putting things into layman's terms
- ☐ Glomming on
- ☐ Talking turkey
- ☐ Countering suspicious queries with "I might ask you the same thing!"
- ☐ Draping earbud cords insouciantly over the back of your neck
- ☐ Pronouncing "insouciant"

☐ Figuring that eating salad makes up for a host of other, nonfood-related sins

- ☐ Going all-out with cockamamie hiccup cures
- ☐ Having minions
- ☐ Lone crusading
- ☐ Asking people if they model
- ☐ Coaxing birds that have gotten inside back outside
- ☐ Saving twist ties
- ☐ Explaining why we're gathered here today
- ☐ Cleaning up at the library book sale
- ☐ Finding treasures at yard sales
- ☐ Guilting people into coming to your reading
- ☐ Sensing when people aren't from around here, and asking them if that's the case
- ☐ Having knacks
- ☐ Getting in shoving matches
- ☐ Self-starting
- ☐ Self-stopping
- ☐ Making jokes based on the inherent humor of the word "pants"
- ☐ Cleaning jars before recycling them
- ☐ Moping
- ☐ Mopping
- ☐ Letting people know when they're so busted
- ☐ Tapping on glass with coins
- ☐ Perusing the free weekly papers in unfamiliar towns

- ☐ Noting when points are moot
- ☐ Asking people if they're joking when you know they aren't
- ☐ Passing along old theater wisdom
- ☐ Only connecting
- ☐ Only disconnecting
- ☐ Saying, "What do you mean 'you people'?"
- ☐ Avoiding the phrase "you people"
- ☐ Mentioning it when elevators are really big or really tiny
- ☐ Letting people know when they should probably get that checked out by a doctor
- ☐ Divorcing and remarrying the same person
- ☐ Taking back what's rightfully yours
- ☐ Having a pretty good sense of what's out there
- ☐ Making people's days
- ☐ Requesting that people make your day
- ☐ Finding tasks to do at volunteer events
- ☐ Preparing a face to meet the faces that you meet
- ☐ Passing self-administered sobriety tests
- ☐ Spouting dogma
- ☐ Walking for cures
- ☐ Biking for cures
- ☐ Doing scientific research for cures

YOU ARE GOOD AT PREPPY THINGS

- ☐ Actually saying, "Tennis, anyone?"

- ☐ Outfitting mudrooms

- ☐ Naming dogs

- ☐ Only showing signs of intoxication when socially appropriate

- ☐ Having spare repp ties on your person

- ☐ Shaving off every trace of facial hair

- ☐ Being stylishly prepared for inclement weather

- ☐ Getting the kids to sing Revolutionary War marching songs in unison

- ☐ Having no fear in the face of cold oceans

- ☐ Casually ascertaining where someone went to college

- ☐ Casually ascertaining where someone went to preschool

- ☐ Casually letting people ascertain where you went to college and preschool

- ☐ Having the good kind of lockjaw

- ☐ Not needing any handbook to tell you how to live, but having one anyway

- [ ] Not being able to read your own handwriting
- [ ] Taking an academic approach
- [ ] Changing your name to something cooler
- [ ] Assuming any compliment delivered within earshot is directed toward you
- [ ] Adjectivizing words (e.g., "homeworky")
- [ ] Crashing parties
- [ ] Mailing posters
- [ ] Keeping drawstrings even
- [ ] Applying the over/under to nonsports situations
- [ ] Writing outlines in proper outline format
- [ ] Taming shrews
- [ ] Letting shrews run wild and free
- [ ] Leaving a little something to the imagination
- [ ] Apologizing for interruptions
- [ ] Concealing erections behind textbooks
- [ ] Shaking sand out of your shoes
- [ ] Enforcing hacky sack decorum
- [ ] Making people nervous
- [ ] Accurately describing your pain on a scale of 1 to 10
- [ ] Coming up with binding theories of the universe
- [ ] Coming up with nonbinding theories of the universe

☐ Being unafraid of using public drinking fountains

- [ ] Recognizing when words are of the fighting variety, and acknowledging them as such
- [ ] Blinging things out
- [ ] Chortling
- [ ] Asking people what their deal is
- [ ] Getting old lighters to work again
- [ ] Keeping things under your hat
- [ ] Complaining about while contributing to a lack of diversity
- [ ] Noting game-changers
- [ ] Supporting the arts
- [ ] Undermining the arts
- [ ] Completing each other's sentences
- [ ] Having things carted off
- [ ] Responding in kind
- [ ] Losing your sunglasses
- [ ] Catching the second half
- [ ] Explaining philosophical concepts through sitcoms
- [ ] Letting people know when they should be ashamed of themselves
- [ ] Shaking your fist at the sky
- [ ] Finding artistic outlets
- [ ] Finding sexual outlets
- [ ] Finding athletic outlets
- [ ] Finding electrical outlets

- ☐ Getting your hands on hard-to-find replacement parts
- ☐ Jumping from rooftop to rooftop
- ☐ Making bold ice cream topping choices
- ☐ Getting reluctant suction cups to stick
- ☐ Crowbarring things open
- ☐ Being booked solid
- ☐ Relentlessly pursuing the new
- ☐ Getting free songs from the jukebox by whacking it with your elbow
- ☐ Having a second childhood
- ☐ Stretching that first childhood out indefinitely
- ☐ Being a friend of the family
- ☐ Being into anime
- ☐ Feeling vaguely bad because you're not into anime
- ☐ Improvising holes so papers fit into three-ring binders
- ☐ Politely getting off the phone with relatives
- ☐ Knowing when a restaurant's bathroom door is locked or just hard to open
- ☐ Not counting books you read for school
- ☐ Inserting ATM cards into slots correctly the first time
- ☐ Remembering whether you took that pill or not
- ☐ Diagnosing strep throat
- ☐ Gazing into the abyss

☐ Sensing when the house rules for the hot tub are okay
  with nudity

- [ ] Really selling it
- [ ] Pretending you didn't just see that
- [ ] Claiming to have solved various secret sauce mysteries
- [ ] Staging reenactments
- [ ] Milling around
- [ ] Averting your eyes
- [ ] Ascending to other realms
- [ ] Sensing if a religious symbol on a necklace indicates a religious faith, a fashion statement, or an ironic comment on religion and fashion
- [ ] Coming up with call-and-response marching chants that are just bawdy enough
- [ ] Taking care not to disrupt a jacket's drape
- [ ] Noting when something just doesn't feel right
- [ ] Noting redundancies
- [ ] Pointing out unnecessary repetitions
- [ ] Remembering what the world was like before the Internet
- [ ] Considering alternate airports
- [ ] Issuing tall orders
- [ ] Knowing when animals are fighting or making love
- [ ] Skewing results
- [ ] Hand-compacting the trash
- [ ] Dressing to kill
- [ ] Dressing to heal

- ☐ Getting stupid
- ☐ Pretending to be overly proud of friends who run the marathon
- ☐ Being in on the joke
- ☐ Dwelling in possibility
- ☐ Dwelling in actuality
- ☐ Personalizing your cubicle
- ☐ Measuring things in terms of football fields
- ☐ Taking pictures of your feet
- ☐ Getting in snits
- ☐ Moseying
- ☐ Gnawing
- ☐ Defusing the tension
- ☐ Ratcheting up the tension
- ☐ Siring heirs
- ☐ Turning things over and over in your mind
- ☐ Turning things over and over in your hand
- ☐ Getting people to go to yoga with you
- ☐ Taking forever to leave the party
- ☐ Having glitter on you but not knowing how it got there
- ☐ Learning new languages as an adult
- ☐ Being mistaken for someone who gives a rat's ass

☐   Eating fruit seductively

- ☐ Being realistic about how great things were even in their heyday
- ☐ Drifting from town to town
- ☐ Staying put
- ☐ Giving people your card
- ☐ Instantly sensing which walls in any structure are load bearing
- ☐ Fanning yourself
- ☐ Keeping the handle of your survival knife stocked
- ☐ Grinning like a maniac
- ☐ Winterizing things
- ☐ Citing old *Far Side* comics
- ☐ Acquiring fun facts
- ☐ Acquiring regular facts
- ☐ Toggling
- ☐ Presoftening butter
- ☐ Making grown men cry
- ☐ Reminding people of things they asked you to remind them about
- ☐ Having epiphanies
- ☐ Making fun of headlines on women's magazines
- ☐ Liquid lunching
- ☐ Having late-night self-doubt sessions
- ☐ Winning free pinball games
- ☐ Knowing who the real victim is here

- ☐ Benefiting from beginner's luck
- ☐ Rooting not for a particular team but for a close contest
- ☐ Scaling back
- ☐ Cocooning
- ☐ Doing the robot
- ☐ Explaining that you're just trying to do your job, ma'am (or sir)
- ☐ Looking innocent
- ☐ Vowing to get back there someday
- ☐ Getting worn-out Velcro replaced
- ☐ Storing sweaters properly
- ☐ Splitting your voice
- ☐ Suggesting banana splits
- ☐ Coining names for new generations
- ☐ Suggesting names for new generations that don't quite catch on (e.g., the Transcendenials!)
- ☐ Heading out
- ☐ Ducking in for a few minutes
- ☐ Copping squats
- ☐ Copping feels
- ☐ Threatening to call the cops
- ☐ Thinking you just saw nipple
- ☐ Peacing out

- [ ] Turning up your collar against the cold
- [ ] Getting away with cowboy boots east of the Mississippi River
- [ ] Actually smacking yourself in the head when you realize you've forgotten something
- [ ] Actually slapping your knee when laughing hard
- [ ] Having stuff that's only available in foreign countries
- [ ] Being the neighbor that other neighbors try to keep up with
- [ ] Choosing drinks that require domed lids
- [ ] Sneaking sweets
- [ ] Thumbing your nose
- [ ] Elbowing your partner
- [ ] Eyeing your opponents
- [ ] Ribbing your buddies
- [ ] Requesting that people join you or die
- [ ] Being open to new ways of doing things
- [ ] Clapping along
- [ ] Getting your requests played for the encore
- [ ] Working the phrase "Even though we may not have always gotten along" into toasts for siblings
- [ ] Strong-arming the PTA
- [ ] Going all out
- [ ] Going all in

☐ Spotting typos

- ☐ Flinging things
- ☐ Knowing when offering a seat to someone will be appreciated rather than seen as insulting
- ☐ Making a good impression on the parents
- ☐ Resisting the urge to give cats literary names
- ☐ Knowing what you can and can't take on passenger planes
- ☐ Being into things before they're cool
- ☐ Being into things that never become cool
- ☐ Asking people if they wanna get hurt
- ☐ Blowing speakers out
- ☐ Coming up with new -illionaire words
- ☐ Transferring calls
- ☐ Turning "You suck" into an affectionate statement
- ☐ Making "dude" gender neutral
- ☐ Requesting permission to rephrase things
- ☐ Knowing when a doll crosses the line from charmingly to creepily realistic
- ☐ Cutting in
- ☐ Swearing you only had one glass of wine
- ☐ Finishing the coleslaw
- ☐ Holding forth on the importance of family
- ☐ Always having a new thing ("It's my new thing!")

- ☐ Having lofty reasons for not wearing a helmet
- ☐ Swallowing pills with only saliva
- ☐ Pushing the limits of "normal wear and tear"
- ☐ Jingling *all* the way
- ☐ Knowing which saw to use
- ☐ Being a calming influence
- ☐ Having a preternatural sense of which part of the store is women's and which is men's
- ☐ Redoubling your efforts
- ☐ Halving your efforts
- ☐ Believing you'll live forever in some form
- ☐ Having funny synonyms for "stole" (e.g., "Somebody G-dogged our stuff!")
- ☐ Using the phrase "Yo, cuz!" when greeting cousins
- ☐ Not losing any board game pieces
- ☐ Threading frayed shoelaces through eyelets
- ☐ Slathering
- ☐ Insisting the seating go girl-boy-girl-boy
- ☐ Making sure everybody's on the same page
- ☐ Comparing things to M. C. Escher drawings
- ☐ Improving steadily
- ☐ Asking people to smell things
- ☐ Eating massive amounts of peanuts

☐ Maintaining the ability to be truly shocked by celebrity misdeeds

- ☐ Spewing quotables
- ☐ Braving portable public toilets
- ☐ Doing things in a stone-cold manner
- ☐ Simplifying, simplifying
- ☐ Exposing dark underbellies
- ☐ Issuing pink bellies
- ☐ Peeling parking violation stickers off of car windows
- ☐ Inventing words that end in -butante (e.g., "guitarbu-tante")
- ☐ Having funny euphemisms for being pregnant
- ☐ Having funny euphemisms for giving birth
- ☐ Pointing out who the real heroes are
- ☐ Having fun on patches of ice
- ☐ Claiming you can quit whenever you want
- ☐ Removing hair from drains without being grossed out
- ☐ Watching your back
- ☐ Washing your back
- ☐ Having artful corn-on-the-cob-eating patterns
- ☐ Utilizing the reversibility of reversible garments
- ☐ Smiling enigmatically at private jokes
- ☐ Remembering why you fell in love in the first place

- [ ] Knowing just how much spin to give your dating profile
- [ ] Muttering under your breath
- [ ] Grumbling about diplomatic immunity
- [ ] Enjoying but not abusing diplomatic immunity
- [ ] Getting self-invented nicknames to stick
- [ ] Knowing which trains are bound for glory
- [ ] Making full use of the balcony
- [ ] Bashing people with fire extinguishers
- [ ] Knowing which fires go with which extinguishers
- [ ] Making a show of thanking bartenders when they ask to see your ID
- [ ] Emptying pockets before doing laundry
- [ ] Collecting exotic matchbooks
- [ ] Not scratching the affected area
- [ ] Defending the fact that your favorite football team is from somewhere other than your hometown
- [ ] Refusing to click through online slideshows
- [ ] Finger-kicking paper triangles through hand-goals
- [ ] Learning a word a day
- [ ] Separating sandwich cookies cleanly
- [ ] Getting people to say what they're thankful for
- [ ] Keeping sunflower seed hulls in your cheek while extracting new seed-meat
- [ ] Writing open letters
- [ ] Projecting an aura of competence

- [ ] Letting movie misquotes slide
- [ ] Thinking of things in terms of man-hours
- [ ] Describing things as "The thinking-man's version" of such-and-such
- [ ] Sending yourself flowers
- [ ] Keeping napkin use to a minimum
- [ ] Knowing when it's time to get your eyeglasses adjusted by a professional
- [ ] Mounting and dismounting ski lifts with grace
- [ ] Saving the day
- [ ] Utilizing the word "utilize"
- [ ] Giving noogies
- [ ] Yelling and clapping when asked to at concerts (All the ladies in the house say, "HEY-YO!")
- [ ] Swooping
- [ ] Knowing which vitamins and minerals are essential
- [ ] Pulling off pinkie rings (as in making them look good)
- [ ] Pulling off pinkie rings (as in removing them)
- [ ] Knowing when you've done all you can do here
- [ ] Opening envelopes neatly with your finger
- [ ] Making a big production out of yawns
- [ ] Avoiding clichés
- [ ] Embracing clichés

☐ Adding "yo" at the end of half your sentences and making it sound natural

- [ ] Explaining your food allergies to servers who don't speak your language
- [ ] Leaning properly while riding on the backs of motorcycles
- [ ] Having nemeses
- [ ] Asking people to "beer" you
- [ ] Knowing your vinegars
- [ ] Describing noses in terms of the natural landscape
- [ ] Taking only what you need
- [ ] Getting high on life
- [ ] Tripping on life
- [ ] Finding posts to scratch your back on
- [ ] Speaking from beyond the grave
- [ ] Breaking glass in case of emergencies
- [ ] Breaking glass whenevs
- [ ] Judging silently
- [ ] Judging audibly
- [ ] Knowing which celebrities are Scientologists
- [ ] Knowing which celebrities are Jewish
- [ ] Knowing which celebrities are gay
- [ ] Knowing which celebrities are vegetarian
- [ ] Knowing which celebrities are short
- [ ] Embracing fad fears

☐ Going on about how you love the smell of books

- ☐ Touching your toes, and making others feel inferior when they can't
- ☐ Being make-out royalty
- ☐ Singing along to songs you've never heard before
- ☐ Playing bad cop
- ☐ Making fun of trend pieces
- ☐ Pushing the use of hazard lights in nonhazardous situations
- ☐ Showing people how it's done
- ☐ Getting your ya-yas out
- ☐ Keeping your ya-yas contained
- ☐ Setting digital watches
- ☐ Flicking earlobes
- ☐ Going on burrito runs
- ☐ Using the word "sexcapade" with a straight face
- ☐ Contesting results
- ☐ Clipping relevant comics and keeping them on display for a really, really long time
- ☐ Calculating time zone differences
- ☐ Using sharpening steels with panache
- ☐ Weirding people out
- ☐ Keeping track
- ☐ Losing track
- ☐ Running laps on the old track at the junior high

- [ ] Arranging for sitters
- [ ] Bounding out of bed
- [ ] Writing up loyalty oaths
- [ ] Belching daintily
- [ ] Belching mightily
- [ ] Belching at will
- [ ] Belching articulately
- [ ] Asking if there's extra credit
- [ ] Coming up with perfect comebacks the next day
- [ ] Cutting people slack
- [ ] Dominating summer camp competitions
- [ ] Declaring yourself a zen master
- [ ] Using the phrase "If that *is* your real name" to comic effect
- [ ] Using the phrase "If that *is* your real name" to dramatic effect
- [ ] Acknowledging the obvious
- [ ] Letting the obvious pass without comment
- [ ] Folding fitted sheets neatly
- [ ] Opening milk cartons neatly
- [ ] Announcing how the deceased "would have wanted it"
- [ ] Pushing the bounds of "fair use"
- [ ] Not being guilted by a hotel's water conservation suggestions
- [ ] Getting serious

- ☐ Preaching to the choir
- ☐ Practicing what you preach
- ☐ Mocking the child beauty-pageant circuit
- ☐ Celebrating the child beauty-pageant circuit
- ☐ Getting celebrities to autograph unexpected objects/body parts
- ☐ Bantering with cashiers
- ☐ Not feeling cheated when it's revealed to have all been a dream
- ☐ Threatening to participate in New Year's polar bear swims
- ☐ Sneakily flipping people off
- ☐ Accumulating nonfunctioning vehicles in your yard
- ☐ Carbo-loading
- ☐ Asking people if they're carbo-loading
- ☐ Wondering why you didn't just fix it sooner
- ☐ Thinking your meatloaf recipe is really something special
- ☐ Bristling at thoughts
- ☐ Quitting before they fire you
- ☐ Dabbing the corners of your mouth with a napkin
- ☐ Using "gesundheit" as a pick-up line
- ☐ Charming snakes
- ☐ Making gutsy calls
- ☐ Seeing how all these things are connected

☐ Maintaining even sideburns

- ☐ Earning, and using, bragging rights
- ☐ Hearing music in the rhythm of everyday talk
- ☐ Doing it, but not overdoing it, with the incense
- ☐ Making only socially conscious graffiti
- ☐ Pointing out that chopped liver is actually really good
- ☐ Returning to form
- ☐ Getting up and out
- ☐ Staying down and in
- ☐ Using hand sanitizer after shaking hands without insulting those you've just shaken hands with
- ☐ Getting coworkers to cover your shift
- ☐ Getting into arguments about professional wrestling
- ☐ De-smudging kitchen counters
- ☐ De-smudging cheeks
- ☐ Setting up cozy nooks
- ☐ Just browsing
- ☐ Always knowing which three states are being referred to by "the tri-state area"
- ☐ Doing homework while watching TV
- ☐ Making napkin bibs
- ☐ Knowing when all-you-can-eat deals aren't actually deals

☐ Taking pictures of yourself that don't look like you took them yourself

- ☐ Guessing which pieces at an art exhibition will be available as postcards at the gift shop
- ☐ Making wish lists
- ☐ Guzzling data
- ☐ Correcting the auto-correct
- ☐ Announcing which part of the song is your favorite
- ☐ Opening things that won't open
- ☐ Closing things that won't close
- ☐ Taking the coward's way out
- ☐ Knowing what to waterproof
- ☐ Complaining about celebrities who you feel haven't done enough to earn the distinction of being a celebrity
- ☐ Wearing extra-fuzzy hats
- ☐ Referring to rounding errors ("You've only kissed 78 people? In my book that's a rounding error!")
- ☐ Getting people to wonder what the heck he or she sees in you
- ☐ Ranking beach bodies
- ☐ Ranking regular bodies
- ☐ Pretending you were singing when you're spotted muttering to yourself
- ☐ Guessing what's behind the censor's bleeps
- ☐ Coming up with "I'd like to simonize his undercarriage" type sayings
- ☐ Not letting free samples guilt you into buying the whole deal

- ☐ Mocking corporate logo changes
- ☐ Sensing whether a limo holds famous people, rich people, newlyweds, or prom kids
- ☐ Attributing personality traits to being a former fat kid
- ☐ Kicking your bag along in airport lines
- ☐ Sallying forth
- ☐ Sallying in place
- ☐ Calling your shots
- ☐ Convincing opponents and observers that you called your shot
- ☐ Signing up for alerts
- ☐ Breaking up ice with your heel
- ☐ Specifying whether you get mad or even
- ☐ Convincing yourself that you're not a fraud
- ☐ Tying bandannas
- ☐ Asking questions at lectures that aren't all about you
- ☐ Ending arguments with, "Let's just say we're both wrong"
- ☐ Smelling skunks first
- ☐ Comically but poignantly mishandling the ashes of loved ones
- ☐ Having "signature" lovemaking moves
- ☐ Having "trademarked" lovemaking moves
- ☐ Getting all your lovemaking moves from the public domain playbook

☐ Committing fully to theme weddings

- ☐ Sensing when you have bad breath
- ☐ Working the phrase "I think I knew that" into discussions of things you don't know
- ☐ Advising college students to major in the hard sciences, when you studied comparative literature
- ☐ Advising youngsters to work in the trades, even though you write TV recaps for a living
- ☐ Cannonballing
- ☐ Spotting openings
- ☐ Taking the full cycle of antibiotics
- ☐ Reminding people how important it is to take all of their antibiotics
- ☐ Shaking your umbrella at people
- ☐ Classing up the joint
- ☐ Making up guest beds
- ☐ Giving permission by saying, "Go nuts"
- ☐ Trashing hotel rooms
- ☐ Scanning crowds for persons of interest
- ☐ Knowing whether it's been done
- ☐ Saving instruction manuals
- ☐ Piercing what was previously thought to be unpierceable
- ☐ Walking down train corridors like you're really going somewhere
- ☐ Reflecting sunlight into eyes with your watch face
- ☐ Sneaking household trash into public trash receptacles

- [ ] Reaching out to old friends
- [ ] Not freaking when old friends reach out to you
- [ ] Mocking people's holiday letters
- [ ] Reading holiday letters with gratitude and affection
- [ ] Reminding everyone that you're not yourself until you've had your morning coffee
- [ ] Making science fair volcanoes
- [ ] Hopping fences
- [ ] Bringing your own seat cushions
- [ ] Always ordering the extra spicy
- [ ] Always ordering the mild
- [ ] Doing dramatic recitations of old sitcom theme songs
- [ ] Working hard and playing hard
- [ ] Knowing when a Dennis is with one or two *n*'s
- [ ] Entering the void
- [ ] Leaving the void
- [ ] Expressing hate for something by saying, "I don't *love* it"
- [ ] Having an inner circle
- [ ] Knowing the difference between a radon alert and a low battery warning
- [ ] Hearing the difference between laugh tracks and live studio audiences
- [ ] Cutting through the park

YOU ARE GOOD AT CRAZY
UNCLE THINGS

- ☐ Having a wanton disregard for whether patterns match
- ☐ Enthusiastically using whiskey as an antiseptic
- ☐ Having a wanton disregard for the drinking age
- ☐ Applying a "seize the day" philosophy in questionable ways
- ☐ Having a wanton disregard for MPAA movie-rating guidelines
- ☐ Having easy-to-find erotica around—printed and electronic
- ☐ Disappearing without explanation
- ☐ Appearing without explanation
- ☐ Rigorously adhering to 1970s-era car seat and bike helmet rules
- ☐ Having unchildproofed coffee table corners
- ☐ Serving three-course meals consisting entirely of frozen pizza
- ☐ Using the Daily Racing Form to teach probability
- ☐ Having a wanton disregard for the concept of bedtime
- ☐ Scratching excessively
- ☐ Always bringing new "special friends" around

- ☐ Picking good places to meet in the mall
- ☐ Sneaking feasts into movie theaters
- ☐ Submitting to a power greater than yourself
- ☐ Embracing the darkness
- ☐ Having some other project that you're working on
- ☐ Giving a full report on your date last night
- ☐ Reminding everyone that you pay taxes
- ☐ Telling people how easy or hard it was to get pregnant
- ☐ Tacking on, "And good for you!"
- ☐ Knowing the best keywords for searches
- ☐ Remembering the names of people's pets
- ☐ Worrying about credit ratings
- ☐ Being ready for a vacation immediately after returning from a vacation
- ☐ Selling yourself short
- ☐ Twisting swizzle sticks into intriguing shapes
- ☐ Issuing disclaimers
- ☐ Helping people find their chakras
- ☐ Announcing that you know when you've been licked
- ☐ Actually sending links to people when you casually tell them you'll send them a link

☐ Not being ashamed to stop and stare upward when visiting cities

- [ ] Dispensing parables about the evils of gossip before gossiping
- [ ] Saying "You're not getting rid of me that easy!" before overstaying events
- [ ] Pulling gloves off one finger at a time
- [ ] Commenting on how small the old high school feels now
- [ ] Knowing which superpower you'd want, if given a choice
- [ ] Tricking people into saying their name when you've forgotten it
- [ ] Really outdoing yourself this time
- [ ] Getting all worked up over nothing
- [ ] Comparing the sports greats of different eras
- [ ] Knowing your nuts
- [ ] Knowing you're nuts
- [ ] Mocking camouflage worn outside of combat
- [ ] Knowing the difference between hurts and hurts so good when giving massages
- [ ] Diligently changing the refrigerator baking soda every 30 days
- [ ] Diligently changing the refrigerator baking soda every 30 years
- [ ] Diligently telling people that keeping baking soda in the refrigerator doesn't do anything
- [ ] Diagnosing people with workaholism
- [ ] Spreading cold butter across toast evenly
- [ ] Dealing with tin cans that don't open completely

- [ ] Determining whether the letters "FBI" on a cap stand for "Federal Bureau of Investigation" or "Female Body Inspector"

- [ ] Taking senior portraits that fully express your character

- [ ] Expressing regional pride through barbecue

- [ ] Knowing how to properly address uniformed soldiers and police

- [ ] Not getting tricked by even really clever spam

- [ ] Not getting fooled by the riddle where it turns out the mom is the doctor

- [ ] Saying "There's no there there"

- [ ] Not getting frustrated when your issue isn't in the FAQ or troubleshooting guide

- [ ] Knowing when you've hit bottom

- [ ] Knowing when you have a ways to go before hitting bottom, and making the most of it

- [ ] Getting people to sign releases

- [ ] Spotting bras masquerading as bikini tops

- [ ] Removing your motorcycle helmet to reveal luxuriant, flowing locks

- [ ] Advocating marijuana as a cure-all

- [ ] Enforcing dibs

- [ ] Boasting about your regularity

- [ ] Consolidating partially eaten dishes while still at the table

- [ ] Announcing that you're consolidating partially eaten dishes

☐ Being a good wingman

- [ ] Taking the magazine from the waiting area into the examination room
- [ ] Always having some new scheme that involves pitching products or sales opportunities at family gatherings
- [ ] Whooping it up
- [ ] Suspecting ghostwriters
- [ ] Not mixing up Iceland and Greenland
- [ ] Pointing out when people misunderstand Nietzsche's concept of the Übermensch
- [ ] Spelling "Nietzsche" correctly without looking it up
- [ ] Shooting hoops in the old gym, after-hours, under a cone of light
- [ ] Hanging tough
- [ ] Hanging weak
- [ ] Just hangin'
- [ ] Telling café workers "Don't bet on horses" and calling it your "tip"
- [ ] Coming up with fictional -istan countries
- [ ] Suggesting that maybe a good rain would wash the scum off these streets
- [ ] Visiting graves
- [ ] Horning in
- [ ] Honing in
- [ ] Taking care not to wear all the same brand
- [ ] Not blowing your top while reading infuriating online comments

☐ Torturing people by not telling them whether you're expecting a girl or a boy

- [ ] Refusing to acknowledge the Dodgers post-Brooklyn
- [ ] Tactfully advising people about what sort of collar their dog should be wearing
- [ ] Basing youthful drug habits on the idea that you might run for president someday
- [ ] Continuing to blame your guidance counselor
- [ ] Embracing an inability to keep houseplants alive as a key part of your identity
- [ ] Buying domain names as soon as you get a vague idea for a business
- [ ] Falling right back into old patterns of behavior
- [ ] Avoiding hospital visits/funerals while not seeming selfish
- [ ] Explaining movie plots without giving away spoilers
- [ ] Pre-empting spoilers from oblivious movie describers
- [ ] Working the phrase "It's not that I don't *trust* you" into discussions where you don't trust somebody
- [ ] Self-deprecating after public stumbles
- [ ] Pushing your way through crowded bars without gathering resentment
- [ ] Getting waitstaff to fix your order without them hating you
- [ ] Getting through airline security without using any bins
- [ ] Seeming smart yet humble while watching *Jeopardy!* in a group
- [ ] Discreetly picking your nose under cover of Kleenex
- [ ] Improvising air fresheners in friends' bathrooms

☐ Pretending to be doing yoga while actually just checking if you remembered the deodorant

- [ ] Not getting comedians started
- [ ] Living in the here and now
- [ ] Living in the there and then
- [ ] Referring to rumspringa, the Amish tradition of sowing wild oats, whenever possible
- [ ] Winning arguments on stamina alone
- [ ] Arguing for things you don't believe in just because you like to argue
- [ ] Knowing the difference between country and alt-country
- [ ] Making red pepper lights your signature decorating flourish
- [ ] Getting restaurant companions to trade meals when you misorder
- [ ] Fitting couches through doorways
- [ ] Knowing how seriously to take the "use by" date
- [ ] Knowing when it's quicker to walk
- [ ] Asking the production assistant what movie they're filming
- [ ] Stabilizing unstable tables
- [ ] Accepting table instability
- [ ] Yelling "Finish him!" when appropriate
- [ ] Predicting when movies will have blooper reels at the end
- [ ] Estimating Scoville heat units of various hot peppers
- [ ] Having a P.O. box
- [ ] Being cool about sharing lip balm

- ☐ Guessing given names behind people's nicknames
- ☐ Taking one big slice of cake rather than ten slivers that add up to way more than a slice
- ☐ Inserting cards and removing them quickly
- ☐ Knowing when things are what they are, and announcing it
- ☐ Providing incisive commentary on red-carpet outfits at awards shows
- ☐ Taking things out of context
- ☐ Policing proper use of the words "literally" and "hopefully"
- ☐ Embracing changes in language
- ☐ Lugging equipment
- ☐ Reminding everyone how you're slowly dying inside
- ☐ Being easy to buy gifts for
- ☐ Leaving tender moments alone
- ☐ Letting people know that they're paying for the label
- ☐ Scraping dog doo completely off shoes using only the curb
- ☐ Saying "intruder alert" in a computer voice
- ☐ Suspecting inside jobs
- ☐ Telling people to apply
- ☐ Starting chants of "Chug . . . chug . . . chug . . ."
- ☐ Having crises of faith

☐ Telling twins apart

- [ ] Reminding people that slurping and belching are considered polite, if not obligatory, in many cultures
- [ ] Announcing that you're not politically correct
- [ ] Letting people know they'll get what's coming to them
- [ ] Throwing and catching tennis balls out the windows of moving cars
- [ ] Pulling illegal U-turns
- [ ] Getting out of requests to help people move
- [ ] Popping dandelions
- [ ] Letting people know when it's a pleasure watching them work
- [ ] Creating personal fiefdoms
- [ ] Detoxing
- [ ] Using coat hooks
- [ ] Fooling dogs about which hand the kibble is in
- [ ] Shooting guns sideways
- [ ] Roaring back
- [ ] Describing nonedibles as "delicious"
- [ ] Working the phrase "Just get over it, already" into informal counseling sessions
- [ ] Having a lot of cousins
- [ ] Getting people to play catch with you
- [ ] Getting people to play chess with you

- [ ] Hitting up people at the office for donations
- [ ] Avoiding people at the office who are good at hitting up people for donations
- [ ] Using war metaphors for disease
- [ ] Accusing volunteers of doing volunteer work for selfish reasons
- [ ] Shying away
- [ ] Knowing the value of a dollar
- [ ] Knowing the difference between a blown speaker and fuzzy reception
- [ ] Saying farewell to youth and beauty
- [ ] Overcompensating
- [ ] Compensating precisely the right amount
- [ ] Pointing out people who "get it"
- [ ] Knowing when to break all the rules
- [ ] Inquiring about group discounts
- [ ] Trying new mind-altering drugs before the DEA gets around to banning them
- [ ] Riffing wittily on superheroes
- [ ] Seeking second opinions
- [ ] Not getting upset when your favorite songs from childhood show up on the oldies station
- [ ] Blurring boundaries
- [ ] Writing reminders on your hand
- [ ] Excluding present company

☐ Hydrating

- [ ] Leaving priceless string instruments in the backs of taxis and having them miraculously returned to you

- [ ] Working the phrase "I'm not wearing any underwear" into casual conversation

- [ ] Recognizing skylines

- [ ] Fearlessly leaning on stranger's cars

- [ ] Tying knots in cherry stems with your tongue

- [ ] Spitting watermelon seeds to competition-length distances

- [ ] Predicting when robots will turn on their makers

- [ ] Waiting for amnesty day to return overdue library books

- [ ] Apologizing for that confusion back there

- [ ] Using the phrase "for realsies" and still having people take you seriously

- [ ] Not overfeeding goldfish

- [ ] Having hatboxes

- [ ] Starting backlashes

- [ ] Convincing people that you're appreciating art for the sake of art, rather than the nudity

- [ ] Coming up with new variations on "piehole" (e.g., "We can go as soon as I butter this and cram it in my toast-hole")

- [ ] Asking friends to do you solids

- [ ] Pushing take-a-penny-tray etiquette to the limit

- [ ] Convincing healthy people to call in sick

- ☐ Knowing when a comeback attempt would only tarnish your legacy
- ☐ Getting restaurants to seat your incomplete party
- ☐ Having pride in your sock-folding technique
- ☐ Having one household chore that you really, really hate
- ☐ Confounding expectations
- ☐ Giving everyone within earshot detailed reports on your most recent bowel movements
- ☐ Not needing the lyrics when doing karaoke
- ☐ Only using "I'm on my way" when you're actually on your way
- ☐ Threatening to go to business school
- ☐ Using shortcut keys
- ☐ Having cool giant maps
- ☐ Gazing into the distance after picking up the newspaper from the driveway
- ☐ Tapping can lids before opening them
- ☐ Handing trash from your seat-neighbor to the flight attendant
- ☐ Collecting change under 25 cents
- ☐ Following soccer in non–World Cup years
- ☐ Unloading similar items from the dishwasher together to maximize efficiency
- ☐ Coming up with new breeds of envy ("I have nostril envy!")

☐ Not waiting until college to find yourself

- [ ] Pointing out when a skill is all in the wrist
- [ ] Reading into things too much
- [ ] Not reading into things enough
- [ ] Micromanaging attempts to get pregnant
- [ ] Threatening to run for the school board
- [ ] Taking what the clown in the dunk tank yells at you personally
- [ ] Knowing when it's cool to get a souvenir T-shirt
- [ ] Calling it in the air
- [ ] Lobbying for the best 2 out of 3
- [ ] Lobbying for the best 3 out of 5
- [ ] Declumping clumped things
- [ ] Intuiting how people like their coffee
- [ ] Always having a different old-fashioned word for "legs"
- [ ] Saying "De-nied!" really dramatically
- [ ] Giving to beggars based on performance rather than perceived need
- [ ] Encouraging people to do things by saying, "You'd be an idiot not to!"
- [ ] Writing notes to self
- [ ] Barely hanging on
- [ ] Taking pride in your cracked smartphone screen
- [ ] Referring to people as "well spoken" without it coming off as an insult

- ☐ Definitively knowing what size drink you want
- ☐ Resealing bags
- ☐ Calling kids "slugger"
- ☐ Figuring out what that comes to per hour
- ☐ Using rubber bands as bracelets
- ☐ Splitting pills
- ☐ Coming up with new signatures
- ☐ Letting people know you dreamed about them without creeping them out
- ☐ Flipping off photographers
- ☐ Using the little buttons on soda cup lids
- ☐ Washing thermoses out thoroughly
- ☐ Making good on "I'm telling you for the last time!" threats
- ☐ Dismissing every idea as pop psychology
- ☐ Dismissing every experimental finding as junk science
- ☐ Using "It pays for itself" to describe things that don't pay for themselves
- ☐ Just blurting it out
- ☐ Viewing the application of sunscreen as a moral issue
- ☐ Assuring people who knock something over that "It happens all the time"
- ☐ Not breaking the laws of civility when trying to acquire the season's hot new toy
- ☐ Pointing out that driving is more hazardous than flying

☐ Spotting stray cats

☐ Being spotted by stray cats

- [ ] Acting like you know what you're talking about
- [ ] Exchanging pleasantries
- [ ] Hoarding pleasantries
- [ ] Being able to answer the question "What's your favorite color?" as an adult
- [ ] Ballparking engagement ring value at a glance
- [ ] Reading billboards out loud
- [ ] Letting it be known when you experience déjà vu
- [ ] Being honest when people ask if you can keep a secret
- [ ] Redeeming "Buy 10 Get 1 Free" cards
- [ ] Gently opening and closing public toilet lids with your foot
- [ ] Hiding behind trees
- [ ] Using "urban" as an ethnic designation
- [ ] Gleefully calling out people who use "urban" as an ethnic designation
- [ ] Pointing out which contemporary figures are as bad as or worse than Hitler
- [ ] Coming up with good pet-death euphemisms for young kids
- [ ] Not assuming everyone who orders the vegetarian dish is a vegetarian
- [ ] Judging people by how they use table salt
- [ ] Being proud of that one weird thing you like ketchup on
- [ ] Appreciating cool breezes
- [ ] Chastising those who don't seem to be appreciating cool breezes enough

- [ ] Asking for permission before kissing
- [ ] Blowing off the "Check Engine" light
- [ ] Speculating that you might've cured cancer if you'd spent less time on some hobby
- [ ] Ribbing people who say they get *Playboy* for the articles, even though that's clearly the case
- [ ] Being honest when taking *Cosmo* quizzes
- [ ] Knocking things before you try them
- [ ] Making people play the "You're getting warmer/colder" game
- [ ] Knowing when it's time to start calling a recurring family event a tradition
- [ ] Knowing just what word to wear across the butt of your sweatpants
- [ ] Finding the trunk and gas cap controls on unfamiliar cars
- [ ] Sharing conspiratorial looks
- [ ] Walking while reading
- [ ] Needing to be convinced of the "authenticity" of any specialty restaurant you eat at
- [ ] Knowing when it's time to pitch in and help blow out somebody else's birthday candles
- [ ] Saying "Everything will be okay" in situations where everything clearly won't be okay
- [ ] Saying "It's all for the best" when it is clearly not all for the best
- [ ] Being highly suggestible
- [ ] Announcing whenever your ears pop

YOU ARE GOOD AT
GRANDPARENT THINGS

☐ Figuring that the grandkids inherited all their good traits from your side of the family

☐ Clipping and sending newspaper articles

☐ Employing passive-aggressive criticism of current child-rearing techniques

☐ Refraining from using contemporary slang so as not to freak out the grandkids

☐ Making college and marriage plans for the embryonic

☐ Proudly showcasing photos completely embarrassing to the person pictured

☐ Buying grandkids more candy in one day than you bought your kids throughout their entire puberty

☐ Making "famous" baked goods

☐ Undoing years of hard-fought, parent-instilled discipline in one beautiful, wild weekend

☐ Rapping

☐ Reducing parents to behaving like children in front of their own children

- ☐ Arranging pillows
- ☐ Setting Vietnam-era montages to songs by groups other than Creedence Clearwater Revival or Buffalo Springfield
- ☐ Accepting and embracing your hair situation
- ☐ Lobbying against self-esteem inflation
- ☐ Complaining about how huge soda sizes have gotten
- ☐ Scavenger hunting
- ☐ Getting people to make pancakes for you
- ☐ Committing misdeeds that the whole class gets punished for
- ☐ Knowing what it is you're a child of (e.g., divorce, the '60s, hip-hop)
- ☐ Relying on one Halloween costume for your entire adult life
- ☐ Walking around with the right amount of vague guilt
- ☐ Agonizing over inconsequential decisions
- ☐ Navigating roundabouts
- ☐ Buying the display model
- ☐ Using the expression "not for nothing"
- ☐ Always knowing someone who's on a cleanse
- ☐ Admiring the motorcycles parked outside
- ☐ Justifying bad behavior by saying, "At least I'm not addicted to drugs!"
- ☐ Justifying outrageous expenses by saying, "At least I'm not spending thousands of dollars on drugs!"

☐ Getting people to come down

- ☐ Passionately favoring one drugstore chain over the others
- ☐ Refusing to relocate
- ☐ Not knowing how good you have it
- ☐ Knowing what school is the Harvard of a particular place ("It's the Harvard of Argentina!")
- ☐ Obtaining rare concert footage
- ☐ Having a favorite supermodel
- ☐ Coming up with good pseudonyms for your online avatars
- ☐ Grasping implications
- ☐ Cheating death
- ☐ Dealing fairly with death
- ☐ Making annoying clicking noises
- ☐ Knowing when ponchos are back in
- ☐ Picking things up with your toes
- ☐ Finding something of equal value for "Buy one get one of equal or lesser value free" deals
- ☐ Cracking knuckles at an alarming volume
- ☐ Using brooms for things other than sweeping (e.g., shooing animals, nudging stuff, banging on the ceiling to quiet upstairs neighbors)
- ☐ Knowing the difference between quiet and too quiet
- ☐ Imagining people's type and level of surprise
- ☐ Requesting that people imagine your surprise

☐ Being humbled by the stars in the night sky

- ☐ Giving makeovers
- ☐ Having a look that is conducive to makeovers
- ☐ Tamping things down
- ☐ Teaching people how to use chopsticks
- ☐ Being honest about which classics you haven't read
- ☐ Casually using the phrase "price point"
- ☐ Letting your potential go unrealized
- ☐ Always taking a free lollipop
- ☐ Admitting you have a problem
- ☐ Denying you have a problem
- ☐ Not wanting to get dragged into this mess
- ☐ Taking pictures of people taking pictures
- ☐ Boasting about being a serial monogamist
- ☐ Christening new music genres by juxtaposing two old ones
- ☐ Announcing that you come in peace
- ☐ Pronouncing neighborhoods not cool anymore
- ☐ Using skateboards as makeshift seats
- ☐ Asking if refills are free
- ☐ Keeping people guessing
- ☐ Wondering how you got here

- ☐ Offering an unvarnished take on things
- ☐ Varnishing your take
- ☐ Using one tube or tub of lip balm until it's finished
- ☐ Peaking early
- ☐ Peeking early
- ☐ Working the phrase "I love you, but . . ." into relationship discussions
- ☐ Keeping handwriting level on unlined paper
- ☐ Messing with the best
- ☐ Zeroing in
- ☐ Convincing your spouse you're in an open marriage
- ☐ Convincing yourself you're in an open marriage
- ☐ Dismissing coursework by asking when you're going to use it in real life
- ☐ Sensing which door leads to the closet, which to the basement, which to the bathroom
- ☐ Wielding tongs
- ☐ Having a strategy for going at big sales
- ☐ Basing your core life metaphors on reaping and sowing, even when you're not sure, in this age of industrial agriculture, what those things mean
- ☐ Knowing when you're supposed to go with or against the grain
- ☐ Organizing sleepover activities
- ☐ Tasting and adjusting seasoning
- ☐ Gargling soulfully

☐ Opening beer bottles with your teeth

☐ Opening bottles of champagne with a sword

☐ Always knowing which bottle caps are twist-offs

☐ Opening bottles with lighters

- ☐ Differentiating between similarly colored areas on map graphs
- ☐ Defringing notebook paper before turning it in
- ☐ Having people around who are willing and able to post bail for you
- ☐ Knowing when talking louder won't make any difference
- ☐ Using body parts to predict rain
- ☐ Neatly opening complex plastic coffee cup lids
- ☐ Tweezing out splinters
- ☐ Soothing fevered brows
- ☐ Discussing brisket recipes
- ☐ Knowing what life's too short for
- ☐ Helpfully letting people know when they should be ashamed of themselves
- ☐ Getting everyone to help you look for a lost contact lens
- ☐ Responding to personal threats with "Yeah? You and what army?"
- ☐ Playing Thanksgiving family football to win
- ☐ Creating diversions
- ☐ Screeching to halts
- ☐ Getting used to it
- ☐ Dismissing smart people as brainiacs
- ☐ Dismissing strong people as muscleheads
- ☐ Dismissing compassionate people as bleeding hearts
- ☐ Dismissing funny people as jokesters

- ☐ Dismissing elections as mere popularity contests
- ☐ Blissing out
- ☐ Blissing in
- ☐ Mastering the brownness dial on the toaster
- ☐ Announcing the official names for groups of animals ("Um, I believe it's known as a *blurb* of fireflies and a *posse* of lizards")
- ☐ Viewing allergies as a sign of weakness
- ☐ Having a precise plan for fixing the college football post-season
- ☐ Knowing what pairs well with what
- ☐ Interrupting to ask which water glass is yours
- ☐ Assuming the pace at which you eat is the correct pace
- ☐ Tracing conversational tangents back to the original subject
- ☐ Sticking to your pack-a-lunch-to-save-money plan
- ☐ Not making your cameos in your own projects too obnoxious
- ☐ Retrieving dropped items from sewers using sticks with gum on the ends
- ☐ Knowing whose email forwards to ignore and whose to embrace
- ☐ Asking whether that's gross or not
- ☐ Getting people to stop snoring without waking them up
- ☐ Communicating clearly whether you mean "dog" or "dawg"

- [ ] Not letting adulthood stop you from using cartoon character bandages
- [ ] Keeping old Yakov Smirnoff bits going
- [ ] Calling in favors
- [ ] Taking "Satisfaction Guaranteed" guarantees seriously
- [ ] Starting off with a joke
- [ ] Giving yourself dramatic temple massages
- [ ] Recognizing when bad behavior is a call for help
- [ ] Noting how great the view is
- [ ] Throwing out statistics really quickly so nobody questions them
- [ ] Timing your ingestion of pot brownies so the drug takes effect at an appropriate time
- [ ] Blowing your bangs out of the way
- [ ] Being prepared to take action when you ask, "Is everything okay?"
- [ ] Letting people know when you think their ride is sweet
- [ ] Not letting "some assembly required" get you down
- [ ] Having an endgame
- [ ] Referring to all mild criticism as getting yelled at
- [ ] Letting pigeons and squirrels get really close to you
- [ ] Doing the right thing, even though you'd rather not
- [ ] Missing the point
- [ ] Knowing when your last tetanus shot was
- [ ] Referring to nonhuman objects as your babies

☐ Keeping your rock-and-roll dreams alive

- ☐ Always pulling over for the scenic overlook
- ☐ Fiddling when you can and working when you should
- ☐ Complaining that they changed their formula
- ☐ Coming up with "Sir Blanks-a-Lot" type nicknames ("Of course Sir Slaps-a-Lot would take her side!")
- ☐ Using the -scape suffix (e.g., the counterscape, the barber-scape, the melonscape)
- ☐ Sensing when people have unresolved mommy and daddy issues, and using them to your advantage
- ☐ Not standing idly by while they badmouth such-and-such
- ☐ Standing idly by
- ☐ Checking to see if you qualify
- ☐ Getting the front desk to move you to a room farther from the ice machine
- ☐ Inhabiting alternate realities
- ☐ Getting your coffee punch card retroactively stamped
- ☐ Penciling people in
- ☐ Expressing disappointment by saying, "Just . . . wow"
- ☐ Reassessing old favorites with a sober eye
- ☐ Dismissing things as too preachy
- ☐ Having a lot of inspirational sayings about failure on hand
- ☐ Getting picked for focus groups
- ☐ Convincing yourself that anything containing "real fruit juice" is healthy
- ☐ Promptly installing software updates

- ☐ Thinking that what you wear while watching sports on TV directly affects the outcome of the game
- ☐ Stepping aside to let the new kids have a crack at it
- ☐ Taking your leisure
- ☐ Flailing
- ☐ Using stilts
- ☐ Explaining why you needed a purebred dog
- ☐ Using spite as a motivator to accomplish great things
- ☐ Remembering that funny thing you said yesterday
- ☐ Letting people know when you like their look
- ☐ Just going ahead and having the procedure done
- ☐ Commanding people to put on a happy face
- ☐ Knowing when you can and can't get away with using the word "curvy"
- ☐ Folding notes
- ☐ Wearing hardhats with business suits
- ☐ Sensing when a fancy car has been leased
- ☐ Being aware of how you appear to others
- ☐ Having elaborate, specific plans for when you win the lottery
- ☐ Knowing when they're just bluffing about cutting the locks off every night
- ☐ Knowing when it's time to turn to your local clergy for advice

- [ ] Being okay with using corporate-generated product nick-names
- [ ] Making arguments that consist of the question, "Whose side are you on, anyway?"
- [ ] Solving your midlife crisis with a radical shift in political views
- [ ] Figuring that "being nice" is an even swap for religious faith
- [ ] Knowing when "xoxo" is too intimate an email signoff
- [ ] Weeping uncontrollably
- [ ] Weeping controllably
- [ ] Being okay with being a member of clubs that are willing to have you
- [ ] Letting people know when you've been praying for them
- [ ] Walking around for a long time with a pebble in your shoe
- [ ] Enacting new austerity measures
- [ ] Knowing when a bait and switch is being pulled
- [ ] Not bumping into poles or people when walking while staring at your handheld device
- [ ] Just feeling sick about the whole thing
- [ ] Knowing how long concerts took to sell out
- [ ] Asking people what they take you for
- [ ] Meeting the mayor
- [ ] Milling around
- [ ] Using "totally" as a modifier

☐ Setting off to find America

YOU ARE GOOD AT COMPLETING SENTENCES!

Okay! I'm convinced! I am good at things! However, exhaustive as this is, you missed a few of my very special skills that don't pay any bills. In fact, one of the things I'm good at is respectfully setting the record _____. Especially by filling in _____.

Telling the difference between _____ and _____, even when blindfolded.

Getting _____ stains out of _____, without using _____.

Training _____ to _____, even though everyone says they are untrainable.

Balancing _____ and _____ without sacrificing _____.

Being aware of the exact level of government-recommended _____ at any given time.

Telling people that they're _____. It's for the greater _____, after all.

Making _____ out of _____.

Keeping _____ in the midst of _____.

Coming up with mathematical proofs for the existence of _____.

Talking people into _____, even when the _____ advises against it.

Having a sixth sense of which _____ has the best _____ while on road trips.

Looking like I just _____, even though I haven't _____ in ages.

Searching for _____ in all the wrong _____.

Adjusting my _____ so no one can tell I'm wearing a _____.

Looking into people's _____ and seeing their true _____. Sometimes I can even tell just by looking at their _____ !

Opening _____ without _____.

Slicing _____ without _____.

Telling people how the humble _____ changed the way America _____.

YOU ARE GOOD AT USING THE "ADDITIONAL NOTES" SECTIONS IN THE BACKS OF BOOKS

Additional Notes:

- [ ] _____
- [ ] _____
- [ ] _____
- [ ] _____
- [ ] _____
- [ ] _____
- [ ] _____
- [ ] _____
- [ ] _____
- [ ] _____
- [ ] _____
- [ ] _____
- [ ] _____
- [ ] _____

☐ _____

☐ _____

☐ _____

☐ _____

☐ _____

☐ _____

☐ _____

☐ _____

☐ _____

☐ _____

☐ _____

☐ _____

☐ _____

☐ _____

☐ _____

☐ _____

☐ _____

☐ _____

☐ _____

☐ _____

☐ _____

☐ _____

☐ _____

☐ _____

ACKNOWLEDGMENTS

I am grateful to my editor at Perigee, Meg Leder. Her enthusiasm for and belief in this project have been strong and unwavering from the start. I'd also like to thank everyone else at Perigee/Penguin who worked on this.

Devin McIntyre at the McIntyre Agency continues to be a great friend, astute shaper of book proposals, and smart negotiator.

My wife, Izzy Grinspan, has been a near-endless source of inspiration and laughs, among other good things. I thank her three times over for her support and tolerance.

The following is some big-tent acknowledging (still, of course, incomplete). It spans from people who gave birth to and raised me, to allies on earlier writing endeavors, to folks who shouted out a good line for this book: Linda Selsberg, Richard Selsberg, Judy Grinspan, Ed Grinspan, Dan Selsberg, Brad Stewart, Ben Karlin, Tom Philipose, Jen Snow, Julie Selsberg, Josh Protass, Kelly Ambrose, Stephen Newhouse, Josh Curnett, Kylie Foxx-McDonald, Ed Park, Erin Cox, Casey Schwartz, Myles Bender, Nancy Beiles, Amanda Hesser, Tad Friend, Lisa Leingang, Chad Gracia, Elaine Selsberg, Steve Selsberg, Paul Joffe, Katia Batchko, Yola Monakhov, Aaron Lubarsky, Scott Dikkers, Sawako Nakayasu, Lauren Bans, Rachel Traub, Lauren Frankfort, Julie Christman, Natasha Leshanski, and Starlee Kine.

PHOTO CREDITS

The people in the photos are models. The captions are intended satirically and do not refer to the persons depicted.

page 2: iStockphoto/Thinkstock
page 5: Creatas Images/Creatas/Thinkstock
page 8: Brand X Pictures/Thinkstock
page 11: Brand X Pictures/Thinkstock
page 14: Hemera/Thinkstock
page 17: Thinkstock Images/Comstock/Thinkstock
page 18: Creatas/Creatas/Thinkstock
page 23: iStockphoto/Thinkstock
page 26: Thinkstock Images/Comstock/Thinkstock
page 29: Hemera/Thinkstock
page 31: Hemera/Thinkstock
page 33: Hemera/Thinkstock
page 35: Ralf Nau/Digital Vision/Thinkstock
page 38: Photos.com/Photos.com/Thinkstock
page 41: Erik Snyder/Photodisc/Thinkstock
page 45: Jupiter Images/Comstock/Thinkstock
page 49: iStockphoto/Thinkstock
page 52: Hemera/Thinkstock
page 54: Hemera/Thinkstock
page 56: Photo by author
page 58: Hemera/Thinkstock
page 60: Jupiter Images/Comstock/Thinkstock
page 61: iStockphoto/Thinkstock
page 63: David De Lossy/Photodisc/Thinkstock
page 66: Hemera/Thinkstock
page 69: iStockphoto/Thinkstock

page 72: iStockphoto/Thinkstock
page 75: Photodisc/Photodisc/Thinkstock
page 78: Hemera/Thinkstock
page 82: iStockphoto/Thinkstock
page 85: iStockphoto/Thinkstock
page 88: Hemera/Thinkstock
page 92: Jupiter Images/Creatas/Thinkstock
page 96: Hemera/Thinkstock
page 99: Digital Vision/Digital Vision/Thinkstock
page 101: Ryan McVay/Photodisc/Thinkstock
page 104: iStockphoto/Thinkstock
page 108: Hemera/AbleStock.com/Thinkstock
page 111: Jupiter Images/Brand X Pictures/Thinkstock
page 114: Hemera/Thinkstock
page 116: Hemera/Thinkstock
page 121: Hemera/Thinkstock
page 126: David De Lossy/Valueline/Thinkstock
page 129: iStockphoto/Thinkstock
page 134: Jupiter Images/Creatas/Thinkstock
page 137: David De Lossy/Valueline/Thinkstock
page 139: Hemera/Thinkstock
page 142: Jupiter Images/BananaStock/Thinkstock
page 145: iStockphoto/Thinkstock
page 149: Photo by author
page 149: Photo by author
page 152: Hemera/Thinkstock
page 156: Hemera/Thinkstock
page 158: Hemera/Thinkstock
page 162: Aidon/Digital Vision/Thinkstock
page 164: iStockphoto/Thinkstock
page 167: Hemera/Thinkstock
page 170: iStockphoto/Thinkstock
page 172: Hemera/Thinkstock
page 175: Hemera/Thinkstock
page 177: Jupiter Images/Brand X Pictures/Thinkstock
page 179: iStockphoto/Thinkstock
page 182: Thinkstock Images/Comstock/Thinkstock
page 185: Hemera/Thinkstock
page 188: iStockphoto/Thinkstock
page 191: Hemera/Thinkstock
page 194: Hemera/Thinkstock
page 196: Hemera/Thinkstock
page 198: iStockphoto/Thinkstock
page 201: Jupiter Images/Comstock/Thinkstock
page 205: Hemera/Thinkstock
page 209: Thinkstock/Comstock/Thinkstock

- [ ] Asking, "Then what?"
- [ ] Standing in a doorway in a reverie and gazing back at a home, classroom, or office, considering all that happened there, as you prepare to leave for the last time
- [ ] Coming up with clever epitaphs
- [ ] Staying through the credits
- [ ] Getting friends who insist on staying through the credits to split early
- [ ] Remembering to get your drink from the roof of the car before taking off
- [ ] Having a signature saying for when you leave a place (e.g., "Gotta jet!")
- [ ] Knowing when to quit
- [ ] Making people say what their favorite part was
- [ ] Looking under the hotel bed before you check out
- [ ] Turning out the lights
- [ ] Cleaning up your area
- [ ] Feeling confident that you turned the stove off
- [ ] Making peace
- [ ] Looking back
- [ ] Looking ahead
- [ ] Enjoying it while it lasts